Photography for Article-Writers

PHOTOGRAPHY FOR ARTICLE-WRITERS

Gordon Wells

ALLISON & BUSBY

An Allison & Busby book
Published in 1990 by
W. H. Allen & Co. Plc
26 Grand Union Centre
338 Ladbroke Grove
London W10

ISBN 0 7490

Phototypeset by Input Typesetting Ltd, London

Printed in Great Britain by

ACKNOWLEDGEMENTS

The author is grateful to the editors of the following
magazines for their permission to reproduce the following
illustrated articles in their printed form:

Figure 3.1 is reproduced from *The Lady*.
Figure 3.2 is reproduced from *Christian Herald*.
Figure 3.3 is reproduced from *TNT* magazine.
Figure 3.4 is reproduced from *Channel Express* (now
defunct).

CONTENTS

INTRODUCTION

This book is NOT for photographers. Nor is it for people who want to become photographers. It is intended for writers who need to illustrate their magazine articles; for writers who wish to remain writers — but want to produce acceptable illustrations that will help to sell their articles.

Let's be even more specific. It is for those writers who normally supply work *on spec* — or who perhaps submit ideas to editors and then supply what they offered. It is not intended for writers who are commissioned by editors to write up specific editorial ideas. (Such commissioned articles will more usually be illustrated by a similarly commissioned photographer working to a very specific editorial brief.)

So the photography we are talking about is not the double-page colour picture of the latest pop star and the accompanying screaming fans; it is not the stilted colour picture of the oh-so-tidy living room of Lady

Windermere; it is not the glamorous exotica of spicy food, nor the frozen flames of the somersaulting racing car. In fact, it's usually not colour at all.

This book is about taking the simple everyday travel picture, or the picture of the collectable artefact; the picture of the unusual signpost, the picturesque clock-tower, or the craftsperson at work. And, although we will look later at the market for colour photography, the type of pictures dealt with will usually be black and white.

The one thing that the above examples of typical article-writers' photographers have in common is . . . they are of interesting or unusual subjects. And that is one of the first lessons to be learnt:

TO SELL, PHOTOGRAPHS MUST BE INTERESTING OR UNUSUAL

Don't take my word for the point about colour, or black and white though. Look for yourself.

Look at almost any general-interest — usually women's — magazine. Look at *SHE*, at *Good House-keeping*, or at *Annabel*. There are often, of course, several big colour features, but these are often of a type normally written on commission. There are usually also several features illustrated with just one or two black and white pictures (or, of course, with no illustrations at all). These latter illustrated features are the ones that most freelance writers will be offering *on spec*.

Look at *The Lady*. This is one of the best markets — ie it takes the largest number of unsolicited contri-butions — for the freelance article-writer. Apart from the front cover, every illustration is in black and white. (We look at *The Lady* in detail, in Chapter 3.)

Look at the newspapers; take *The Guardian* for

instance. Evaluate the opportunities — eg for travel articles in the weekend edition. All illustrations are in black and white.

Look at your local county magazine — always a good market for unsolicited freelance articles. Again, the cover may be a colour picture and some of the main features may have colour illustrations, but many other features will be illustrated exclusively with black and white photographs.

Look at any craft magazine. Most have relatively small circulations, and few big advertisers to bolster up the production costs. Often, they cannot afford to use colour. Certainly, many take only black and white illustrations.

So . . . forget colour photography. At least, for the time being.

The 'package' concept

Editors welcome articles that come complete with illustrations. The writer who can provide the editor with a complete 'package' is off to a head start. Provision of such a package means that the editor doesn't need to search around for relevant pictures to go with the words. From the writer's point of view, the bigger spread of words and pictures make a better-looking feature; the author is more likely to get noticed. (And perhaps asked to do other work.)

Some editors indeed pay for words and pictures at a 'package rate' — so much per page, whether filled with words or with pictures. And, in such cases, the picture fills the space of at least two hundred words — and is often easier to produce.

Another 'words versus pictures' consideration is the

rights you are selling. When you sell an article, you sell the *first* reproduction right; this is then gone forever (and there are very few opportunities for selling *second* reproduction rights). When you sell a photograph though, you are normally only selling the right to a *single* reproduction of it. You can keep on selling the same picture again and again; and all it costs you is the print processing.

(That said, few successful article-writers are much bothered at the loss of first British serial rights (FBSR); exactly the *same* article would not be right for another magazine anyway. The subject of the article can always be written up again, with a different 'slant', a different 'approach' — there is no copyright in facts — and a second FBSR sold, with some of the same photographs perhaps. I shall refer later to the several illustrated articles I have written: *all* about dragons.)

Some editors will not even consider articles at all without accompanying illustrations. (Non-photo-graphically-minded writers can often get around this requirement by asking tourist offices and the like for publicity pictures — for free.) But the real answer — for *any* writer — is to take your own photographs.

It's easy

The good news is that — nowadays at least, and AT THIS LEVEL — photography is easy. In this book you will learn how to take *adequate* — ie 'saleable' in the context of an accompanying feature article — photographs.

If you later find you yearn to become a better, more 'artistic' photographer, there are many good books around. And you might usefully join your local camera club.

The next thing to acknowledge is that black and white photography is not cheap. Rather the reverse. If in the past, you have taken 'happy snaps' on holiday and got the prints back, with a 'free' film thrown in, all for well under a fiver, prepare for a shock. Black and white photography costs much more than colour.

You cannot just pop your black and white film into a prepaid mailing envelope with a cheque and get your 'Super En-prints' back a week or so later. The really big colour film processors won't handle black and white film at all. They are geared up to process hundreds of 'happy snap' films automatically. And nowadays, 'happy snaps' are colour prints. For black and white film processing you need to go to specialist processors. Or there is one black and white film which can — sometimes — be processed by the 'production-line' colour film processors. (*See* Chapter 4.)

In this book, we shall be looking at the various types of camera available — and recommending the simplest possible camera to do the job (the job of the writer needing illustrations). We shall look at some of the 'add-ons' — for photographers as a group, are more prone than most to collecting extra pieces of equipment — and recommending the minimum necessary. (And the minimum necessary is strictly minimal, so fear not.) You won't even need a 'gadget bag' to carry it all in.

And we shall explain, very simply, how a camera works and how you get from 'point and click' to a publishable illustration.

We can't turn you into skilled and artistic professional photographers. For that, among other things, you need a 'seeing eye', an 'eye for a good picture', for 'the moment of truth'. Maybe you have that gift. If so, work on it. Nothing recommended in this book will hamper your inborn ability — and you probably don't need my advice anyway.

This book though is for all the other writers-turned-would-be-photographers — hereafter, 'writer-photographers' — who just need to be able to produce a reasonable picture. This book will explain some of the basic rules of composition, of *framing* a good picture, and of producing a photograph of good technical quality.

Saleable pictures

Some types of picture are more saleable than others. But there are few hard and fast rules. (If there were, every picture I take would be saleable. This is far from the case. I take my share of flops too.) What we can do in this book is to review the types of photograph most likely to be of use to the non-fiction writer. And you will often find that a set of linked photographs will also spark off a new idea for an article.

Certainly, there are some types of photograph that the writer *should not* waste time attempting. Few writer-photographers will be able — or would wish — to produce 'Page 3' type glamour photographs. Nor is this necessary. There are also other fields which you do not need to explore. Remember, you are primarily a writer.

There are right ways and wrong ways of submitting photographs to magazine editors; this book will tell you how to do it the right way. There is a skill in writing a good caption; this is explained. You will be able to do it properly.

If you 'get hooked' on photography, you may want to get more and more involved. Processing your own black and white film is not beyond the ability of any writer; it takes time that might be better spent writing, but against that, it will save money. Processing your prints too is possible — but here the time aspect is even more relevant.

And then you might want to dabble with colour photography. Dabbling is out. Colour photography for magazine use is a highly skilled and specialised art. Colour prints are of virtually no use whatever to a writer. You will have to take colour transparencies if you have visions of selling them. The potential market — and the necessary equipment — for simple colour photography are reviewed. Basically though, don't bother for a while.

Remember, at the level needed for producing saleable black and white photographs for illustrating articles — it's easy.

Let me show you how.

1

THE BASIC PRINCIPLES

Having explained that, today, photography is easy, let us look at what it's all about. It is easier to use a camera well if you understand — very broadly — the basic principles of the photographic process.

And I promise to keep it simple; you won't find it hard to understand.

At its simplest, photography merely requires a light-tight box with a controllable 'hole' through which light can enter, and a piece of light-sensitive film. Indeed, it is possible to take a photograph with a pin-hole camera: a light-proof box with a pin-hole to let the light in. This might have been an interesting experiment at the start of the century when cut film (and film-holders) was available from enthusiastic chemist's shops; today, it is rather pointless — and difficult to set up.

The pin-hole idea however does make it easier to understand the *form* in which the picture gets onto the film.

Think therefore, of a pin-hole camera pointing at a person. The person's face reflects light. That light travels in a straight line, from the face to the pin-hole. Because the face is above the level of the 'camera', the light passes through the hole from the top — and therefore strikes the film at the back of the camera *at the bottom*. In the same way, the lesser amount of light reflected from the person's shoes comes up towards the camera and strikes the film *at the top*. The image is inverted by the pin-hole. And exactly the same thing happens in a proper camera.

Nowadays, cameras have lenses. The lens serves to concentrate — to focus — the light which enters the light-tight camera. And the film now comes in rolls (or on a revolving disc). But rays of reflected light still enter the camera and create an inverted image on a light-sensitive film.

It is all very well creating an image on a piece of light-sensitive film inside a light-tight box. But you, the photographer, want a permanent record of the picture you have captured. To make permanent the image on the film, the film has to be *processed*. We will look at film processing in some detail in Chapter 4 — but it is unimportant unless you want to develop an interest.

Exposure

The next concept we need to explore is *exposure*. A few years ago, people used to worry about 'getting the exposure right' for their photographs. Unless you wish to, you won't need to bother about exposure nowadays, but it helps if you understand it.

If you peer into a dark cupboard — or enter a darkened room — you find it hard to see; you may stare

9

with wider-than-normal open eyes. There is not much light about. Now imagine you are at the seaside, looking out to sea on a bright sunny day. You will shield your eyes, screw them up or shade them — or wear a pair of sunglasses. There is a lot of light about.

Think again about the pin-hole camera with its piece of light-sensitive film. Pointing the 'camera' at the sea would mean a lot of light reflecting back through the pin-hole and onto the film. Envisage now, the same 'camera' and the same piece of film, pointing into the dark cupboard. This time, there would be very little light reflecting through the pin-hold and onto the film.

If you wanted to capture a reasonable image in both situations you would need to vary the amount of light striking the film. And this can be done in two different ways:

- by varying the size of the pin-hole through which the light passes — widening or narrowing the eye;
- by varying the time for which the pin-hole allows light to enter — as in peering, or looking away.

(The amount of light striking the film can also be varied by 'putting on sun-glasses' — by interposing a filter in the path of the reflected light — but this need not concern us yet.)

Apertures

In practice, camera lenses have variable *apertures* — the means of controlling the size of the opening through which the light rays pass. And the cameras — or the lenses themselves — have *shutters* which control the time for which the lens is open.

Camera apertures are measured in what are known as f-numbers. Look at the lens on almost any camera: you will see some sort of expression like f/1.4 or 1:3.5 or, like my own, f/3.3–4.5 (It's a zoom lens.) These numbers are from a standard sequence of 'lens openings' which run: f1.0, f1.4, f2, f2.8, f4, f5.6, f8, f11, f16, f22, f32. You will find some part of this sequence of numbers around the rim of all manually-adjustable lenses. They represent, in fact, measures of the 'lens openings', the apertures; the light-passing facility of each successfully f-numbered aperture is half that of its predecessor.

But not all lenses can be made — at the required price — to fit precisely within that sequence; therefore many lenses are — very roughly — slotted in between the 'proper' f-number sequence. For example, the very popular f3.5 lens.

The f-number marked on a lens is the maximum possible opening of that lens. But virtually all lenses have the facility to reduce their maximum aperture. (In the simplest cameras, a shield with a smaller hole moves across the lens; in more sophisticated cameras, a number of overlapping leaves are made to move, gradually reducing the aperture.) The aperture reduction is usually measured in terms of the f-number sequence. And, as we now know, the low f-numbers are the biggest openings and the high f-numbers, the smallest.

Shutter speeds

The other way of controlling the amount of light reaching the light-sensitive film in the camera is by varying the time for which the aperture is open. Although

11

the films used in early cameras required long time exposures — measured in minutes even — this is not the situation today. Exposure times today are measured in fractions of a second. A one-second exposure is a really long one.

Today's cameras control the time for which the lens is open with their *shutters*. A camera has either a leaf type shutter — wherein a number of leaves, positioned within the lens itself, very quickly rotate open and shut — or a blind, or shield, in front of the film which momentarily moves away.

In the same way that apertures increase or decrease by a factor of two — halving or doubling — shutter speeds, too, operate to a doubling or halving sequence. A commonly used shutter speed sequence is often: 1/1000, 1/500, 1/250, 1/125, 1/60, 1/30, 1/15, 1/8, 1/4, 1/2, and 1 second.

As you can now appreciate, an appropriate exposure could be described as 1/250 second at f8. And if the light then worsened, you can appreciate that changing that exposure to 1/250 sec at f5.6 (doubling the aperture) might suffice to correct for this. Alternatively, and with exactly the same effect, we could change the exposure to 1/125 sec at f8 (doubling the time for which the light could read the film).

To extend that concept, each of the following aperture/shutter speed combinations provides an identical exposure:

fast shutter speed 1/1000 sec at f2.8 wide aperture
1/500 sec at f4
1/250 sec at f5.6
1/125 sec at f8
1/60 sec at f11
1/30 sec at f16

slow shutter speed   1/15 sec at f22 small aperture

And this leads us on to contemplate why one might prefer a faster shutter speed or a smaller aperture.

The shutter speed first — it's the easiest to explain and understand. There are two reasons for preferring a faster shutter speed:

- to 'stop' a moving picture, or
- to reduce the likelihood of 'camera shake' blurring the picture

Everyone has seen newspaper photographs of racing cars stopped in mid-picture; this can be achieved by a very fast shutter speed — or by what is called 'panning' the camera, moving it quickly round, following the subject. Panning' too requires a fast shutter speed — but not quite so fast as for a 'frozen action' shot.

If you look in the more pictorially adventurous, or artistic, publications you will also sometimes see pictures where the subject is allowed to move. This results in a blurred picture which can convey a good impression of movement. For this type of picture a slow shutter speed is used.

The writer-photographer should seldom consider deliberately producing a blurred-action picture — other than for fun. Editors interested in words-and-pictures packages want sharp, rather than artistic, pictures (*see* Chapters 2 and 3).

Of more importance to the writer-photographer is the use of faster shutter speeds to avoid the effects of shaky hands and wobbly cameras. Within the limitations imposed by the frequent need for a small aperture (*see* below), you should always use the fastest possible shutter speed.

Depth of field

Now, the reasons for selecting different apertures. To understand this, we must first think about focussing.

Take a magnifying glass — or borrow a pair of spectacles from a friend for a couple of moments — and look through (just one lens) at your hand. You will find that your hand is only really 'sharp' and clear when the lens is at just one correct distance from it. Close to that 'correct distance' (the point of focus), your hand is fairly sharp; with the lens close to your hand or far from it, your hand is very blurry.

Note particularly that around the 'correct distance' there is a zone (of distances from the hand — the subject — to the lens) of relatively acceptable sharpness.

If we put two or more single glass lenses together, it is possible to adjust their position relative to each other, such that wherever the subject (your hand) is, that can be the point of focus — the 'correct distance' for it to appear sharp. The adjustment of the relative position of the individual elements within a combined lens *focuses* the lens.

Just as, with the single lens, there is a zone of acceptable sharpness around the point of focus, so too is there such a zone with a multiple-element lens. This zone of acceptable sharpness is called the *depth of field*. The zone of acceptable sharpness extends further beyond the point of actual focus than it does in front.

The point of focus does not vary, but the smaller the aperture, the greater the depth of field. Wide open, an f/1.4 lens focussed on a nearby subject will have a very shallow depth of field; stopped down to say f/11, the depth of field increases considerably. The depth of field also varies with the nearness of the subject. The same lens, wide open, focussed on a distant subject will have a large depth of field from some way in front of the subject right back to infinity.

(Simple, fixed-focus cameras, *see* below, make use of the depth of field of their lenses to produce acceptable pictures without specific focussing. The lenses are pre-focussed (fixed-focussed) — at what is called the *hyper-focal distance* — to produce the greatest possible depth of field at an average aperture.)

The wider the angle of the lens — and we will explain wide-angle and telephoto lenses later — the greater the depth of field. This too is also of importance to the designers of simpler cameras. By using a wide-angle lens they reduce the need for focussing.

So . . . the photographer pondering on the most appropriate combination of shutter speed and lens aperture needs to think about how much depth of field the picture requires.

If the picture is of a single or physically flat subject (a statue or plaque for instance), there is little need for much depth of field; conversely, a crowd scene or landscape, with interest in the foreground, the middle distance and the background, requires the greatest possible depth of field. The landscape needs a small ('stopped down') aperture; the single or flat subject does not. (The crowd scene might also require a fast shutter speed; a balance has then to be struck between depth of field and stopped action.)

A shallow depth of field can also be used deliberately to put a background out of focus, thereby concentrating attention on a closer, sharply-focussed, subject. (Achieve this by using a wide aperture and a faster shutter-speed.)

Film

So far, we have looked at ways of controlling the amount of light striking a film inside a camera. For a given subject there remains therefore only one more variable — the film itself. Some films are more sensitive to a given amount of light than others. We say a film is 'fast' if it requires less light to save the same image — and 'slow' if it requires more. That is, there are fast films and slow films.

A film's speed is indicated by the ISO number marked on its box and/or cassette. (Films have long been graded by ASA numbers or by degrees DIN — ASA, American and DIN, continental European — but it is now customary to use ISO — International Standards Organisation — numbers. ISO numbers are usually expressed as two numbers, eg 100/21, which are in fact 100 ASA/21 degrees DIN.) You need only concern yourself with the initial number — the (ASA) 100 in the above instance.

In the ISO/ASA numbering system the film-speed relationship is strictly numerical: a 100 ISO film is twice as fast as a 50 ISO film and a quarter the speed of a 400 ISO film. For example, a subject requiring a shutter speed and aperture setting of 1/125 sec at f/5.6 with a 100 ISO film would require a shutter speed/aperture setting of 1/60 sec at f/5.6 (or 1/125 sec at f/4) with 50 150 film. If the camera were loaded with 400 ISO film, the identical subject could be captured with a setting of, say, 1/250 sec at f/8.

(In the DIN system, a film with half the speed drops 3 degrees DIN and one four times faster would be 6 degrees higher. Every 3 degrees up or down doubles or halves the film speed. The ASA system is simpler.)

There is inevitably a small penalty to pay for faster

film speed. The faster the film, the 'grainier' it is. 'Grain' refers to the size of the clumps of silver compound which form the image on the processed film. Excessive grain makes the resultant picture look 'dotty' — like an old newspaper photograph.

For many writer-photographer purposes, it is best to choose a medium-slow (100 ISO) film. But many photographers standardise on 400 ISO film — for the convenience of a shake-free, faster shutter speed and/or the greater depth of field from a smaller aperture.

One final point about the film. For black and white (and colour print) photography the film records the darkest image where the light is brightest (white) and blank (transparent) where there is least light — ie, where it is dark. In other words, the real-life lighting situation is reversed. The processed pictures are therefore known as negatives.

The negatives are then later printed onto photographic paper which again reverses the image; and we are back where we started, with black blacks and white whites. And, of course, with greys in between.

And that is all the basic principles that any writer-photographer need bother about. (Indeed, you don't need to worry if you haven't quite understood it all. But I shall be upset as that implies I have not explained sufficiently simply.)

Choice of camera

Now we can look at the camera itself. Cameras are categorised basically by their film size. Camera film sizes range from the tiny negative of the (fairly) recent disc camera, through the thumb-nail size of the 110 camera, to the double-postage-stamp size of the 35 mm camera, and on through the credit card (or two-thirds card-sized) size of the 120 roll-film camera to the sky's-the-limit-sized sheet film of the studio camera.

(There are also cameras made by Polaroid — and Kodak — which produce virtually instant pictures. These are useful, when travelling in remote areas of the world, for mollifying the awe-struck natives — if any still exist — by producing immediate complimentary pictures of them. These cameras are of no importance though, to the writer-photographer staying in civilised parts. Editors will not normally consider Polaroid pictures.)

Because editors require the photographs submitted to them to be of a good size, they have to be *enlarged* from the negatives created in the camera. (They are generally required to be at least 7 inches by 5 inches, and preferably 10 inches by 8 inches — *see* later, Chapter 5.) And, largely because of the grain — the clumps of silver compound mentioned earlier — of the films, the greater the degree of enlargement, the poorer the quality of the final print.

It is too much to expect to produce acceptable quality prints of the necessary size from either disc or 110 film. These cameras are quite definitely not suitable for writer-photographer use. Reserve them for taking 'happy snaps'.

At the other extreme, a sheet-film camera is far too big and bulky to be a realistic choice for an ordinary everyday writer-photographer. Not only that, the film costs a lot too. (The negatives will be excellent — but unjustified.)

The 120-size roll-film camera is an excellent choice for writer-photographers — but:

- virtually all 120 roll-film cameras are expensive —

both to buy and to use; (a 12-exposure roll of 120 film costs only about 10 per cent less than a 20-exposure roll of 35 mm film of like quality.)

- 120 roll-film cameras tend to be rather big (and therefore heavy) — the smallest (and the most expensive) are about a 5-inch cube;
- alternative lenses for 120 roll-film cameras are extremely expensive — and not all 120 film cameras can accommodate them.

(If you get around to extending your photography endeavours into taking a lot of colour — *see* Chapter 7 — you will probably find it useful to invest in a 120 roll-film camera. But not otherwise.)

There is no doubt that the most suitable camera size for a writer-photographer is a (full-frame) 35 mm camera. (The qualification about full-frame is because a few 35 mm cameras take 'half-frame' negatives — single-postage-stamp-size — but these too are probably too small to give good quality enlargements.)

The 35 mm camera comes, nowadays, in two basic types: the single-lens reflex camera and the 'compact'. (Some years ago — when I started in photography — virtually all 35 mm cameras were rangefinder cameras; that is, they were focussed by the use of a built-in, lens-coupled rangefinder, rather than by the user judging the sharpness of the picture on a screen as with the conventional reflex camera.) And the boundaries between different types of 35 mm camera are getting fuzzier every day.

(It is still possible — if you are very wealthy — to acquire a top quality 35 mm rangefinder camera. This is the famous Leica. But it is not recommended for ordinary writer-photographers.)

We will comment later on how the boundaries of the

present two basic 35 mm camera types are getting fuzzy. First though, let us take a detailed look at the conventional single-lens reflex and the compact.

The single-lens reflex camera is so named to distinguish it from the once popular twin-lens reflex 120 roll-film camera (typically, and then 'the best', the lovely Rolleiflex).

The single-lens reflex camera (hereafter abbreviated simply to SLR) is not restricted to a single lens. Just to one at a time. It works on the principle of the user actually looking *through the lens* before the picture is taken.

This is achieved by interposing, between the film and the lens, a mirror inclined at 45 degrees; this mirror reflects the picture onto a ground-glass screen at the top of the camera. When ready to expose the film and take the picture — ie, when the picture is 'composed' and focussed — the mirror swings up to cover the screen, making it light-tight. The camera's shutter is then released (opened) and the film is exposed. The mirror then swings back down again, ready for the next picture to be composed.

Very early reflex cameras required the photographer to peer down at the aforementioned ground-glass screen. (This made photographing moving objects somewhat confusing.) In such a state, the reflex camera was, understandably, not as enormously popular as it is today. Then came the pentaprism.

The pentaprism (and this is best understood by looking at the diagrammatic representation at Figure 1.1) sits on top of the SLR's ground-glass screen. It bends the rays of light so that, looking straight ahead, the photographer sees exactly what is on the ground glass. The photographer can thus focus and compose without confusion or inconvenience. (In word-processing terms

20

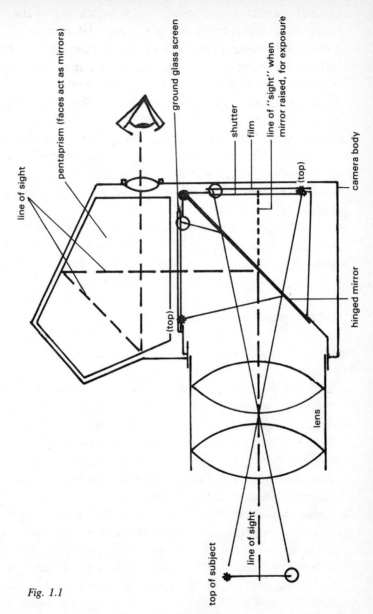

Fig. 1.1

The basic principles of the single-lens reflex camera (the SLR).

21

familiar to many writers, the SLR is a truly WYSIWYG – *what you see is what you get* – camera.)

Once the pentaprism was invented, the days of the manual rangefinder camera were numbered.

The other characteristic of the SLR — closely associated with its WYSIWYG characteristic — is the easy interchangeability of the lenses. You can unscrew (sometimes with an actual screw thread, sometimes with a bayonet lock) the 'standard' lens and replace it with a telephoto or a wide-angle lens. And as soon as you fit the new lens, the view on the ground-glass screen accurately reflects (sorry) the view through the new lens. (That was never possible with the rangefinder camera, which had to resort to add-on viewfinders or to smaller-frame dotted lines within the existing finder.)

Interchangeable lenses

Let us now think about interchangeable lenses.

The 'standard' lens (ie, that with which it is usually sold) on the SLR is usually one with a 50 mm focal length — which means that it has a field of view of about 46 degrees. This field of view is said to be approximately the same as the human eye. (But we don't so specifically restrict our personal view; we move our heads, we glimpse things just outside our view. The camera-user has to be more precise; the negative size is fixed.)

If the photographer wishes to broaden the view of the camera — perhaps to picture a room within which it is not possible to move further back — a wide-angle lens is the answer. Most wide-angle lenses have a focal length of either 28 mm or 35 mm — giving fields of view of 75 and 64 degrees respectively. (There are wide-angle lenses with shorter focal lengths and correspondingly wider views but they are both expensive and liable to give a distorted picture.)

It may help to appreciate the different fields of view by thinking about the width of a horizontal picture (never mind the quality, consider the width) that can be taken from a distance of say ten feet. A 50 mm 'standard' lens covers about a seven feet width at ten feet distance. From the same spot, a 35 mm lens will cover about a ten feet width and a 28 mm lens about twelve-and-a-half feet. And in each case, the height of the picture will, of course, be two-thirds of the width.

Lenses of less than double the 'standard' focal length are usually referred to as long-focus lenses. These are usually of either 70 mm or 85 mm focal length. Long-focus lenses are particularly useful for portrait use. If you take a portrait with either a wide-angle or standard lens it will either be too far away and small, or the facial characteristics may be slightly distorted. The long-focus lens allows the photographer to get just that bit further away, avoiding distortion while capturing a respectably large image on film.

To extend the 'width impression', a 70 mm lens covers a width of just over five feet at ten feet distance and an 85 mm lens covers about four feet.

Lenses with a focal length of about 135 mm and upwards are referred to as telephoto lenses. They bring the subject close to the viewer — and in consequence, they have an increasingly narrow field of view. A 135 mm lens has a field of view of eighteen degrees; a longer, more 'powerful' — and much more expensive — 300 mm lens has a field of only eight degrees. (With telephoto lenses, the ten-foot-distance 'width impression' is no longer relevant. The 135 mm lens already covers less than three feet width in a horizontal picture.)

There is another group of lenses of particular importance — that again would have been impossible to link to a rangefinder camera. This group is the *zoom* lenses.

A zoom lens is capable of changing focal length; the lens 'zooms' in and out — just like on the TV. A single zoom lens can cover everything from a wide-angle to a long-focus view, or from a long-focus view to a tele-photo view. The most popular zoom lenses are the 70–200 mm zoom — but of almost equal popularity is the wide-angle — long-focus zoom, the 28–85 mm or the 35–70 mm. The latter zoom lens, the wide-angle — long-focus one, is a sensible replacement for the standard 50 mm one — which view, it of course embraces.

There are a few disadvantages with zoom lenses. Their optical quality is not always quite as high as that of the single focal length lens — compromises inevitably having to be made. But this reduction in quality is not really significant in everyday use.

Zoom lenses also usually have smaller apertures than comparable single-purpose lenses, (Most popular 35–70 mm lenses have a maximum aperture of f/3.5; a comparably inexpensive single-purpose 50 mm lens would have a maximum aperture of f/1.8.) And, as a result of their design, zoom lenses have a varying maximum aperture: as the elements are moved within the lens to extend its focal length, so too is the maximum aperture reduced. (With one 35–70 mm 'standard zoom' lens, the maximum aperture is f/3.5 at 35 mm reducing to f/4.5 at 70 mm.)

The need for a wide aperture, 'fast' lens is very limited in general photography. Today, there are faster films that can be used without a significant sacrifice of picture (grain) quality. And in many situations, flash is an additional, acceptable, alternative.

The caricature of a 'camera buff' is a man (yes, it's always a man) with a large gadget bag on his shoulder, who is changing lenses at the precise moment when the one unrepeatable picture passes by. If he isn't changing lenses, he is fully occupied in focussing a huge tele-photo. Or he is fitting on a flash gun. And he may well have two or three cameras strung round his neck. Those images are all too often true to life.

The writer-photographer, however, will seldom need much in the way of different lenses. The writer-pho-tographer is not in the business of grabbing a candid close-up of a member of the Royal family. The writer-photographer doesn't need to picture a motor race crash. The writer-photographer can usually get close to his/her subject.

In my view if, as a writer-photographer, you decide on a SLR, you can handle more than 90 per cent of the shots you want with a standard lens plus perhaps a wide-angle. My own preference is for a single zoom lens, ranging from a wide-angle to long-focus. In the past I used a 28–85 mm zoom; today though, I have a 35–70 mm zoom — it is more compact and I have not (yet) discovered anything lacking in its scope.

The compact camera

But enough, for the moment, about the SLR. The other basic type of 35 mm camera is what is nowadays known as a 'compact'. In essence, a compact 35 mm camera is a fixed lens camera needing few adjustments by the user.

A typical simple compact camera would have a 35

mm lens: ie, a wide-angle lens with, as we have seen above, a large depth of field. At the lower end of the range, the lens would be fixed focus — pre-focussed to give the maximum depth of field. It might have a means of changing the lens aperture — with symbols for bright sun, cloudy, or dull — but some simpler cameras don't even have this. Almost all though, will have a built-in electronic flash. In all, the simplest compact camera is no more than an old-fashioned 'Box Brownie' but with 35 mm film — and a flash.

(The drop in price of an electronic flash, and its greater miniaturization — enabling it to be built into the camera body — were major factors in the growth of popularity of the compact camera. With flash, the 'happy snap' is always 'acceptable'.)

With the passage of time though — ie with the development of more and more electronic aids — and with just a few more pounds spent on the camera, far greater sophistication is available. And this increased sophistication has not meant losing the very important simplicity of the compact camera.

For around forty to fifty pounds it is now possible to buy a compact camera with the following features:

- fixed focus 35 mm wide-angle lens
- automatic exposure control
- automatic flash when light level falls
- automatic, drop-in, film loading
- automatic film advance and rewind
- automatic double-exposure prevention
- automatic lens cover.

For just a few more pounds, the following additional features become standard:

- automatic focussing
- automatic film speed identification (by DX coding).

Thereafter, as you spend more money, it is possible to get compact cameras with:

- built-in wide-angle and long-focus lens facility — extra lens elements are added within the camera, to convert the wide-angle lens to long-focus;
- built-in and electrically controlled wide-angle to long-focus zoom lens (usually 35–70 mm);
- close-up focussing facility ('macro') — down to about 2 feet or 0.6 metres distance;
- adjustment for fill-in flash and for exposure of back-lit subjects.

It is clear that, with the most sophisticated compacts, you have a camera capable of dealing with virtually every situation. Without doubt, almost any writer-photographer could be well satisfied with the top-level compacts.

But an average writer-photographer does not even need as much sophistication as the zoom lenses etc. Some writer-photographers would find the switches and buttons that accompany the extra sophistication worryingly over-complicated. A simpler compact would meet most of their needs.

The most important features I would myself look for in a compact camera today would be:

- a single good quality 35 mm lens, ideally capable of close-up (macro) photography and of long exposures in low-light conditions:
- automatic film speed identification (DX coding);
- automatic exposure control — ideally with means

of back-light adjustment and compensation for fill-in flash;

- automatic focussing;
- a built-in flash *that can be switched off*. (There are many indoor photo opportunities where flash is forbidden — yet worthwhile pictures can still be obtained.)

You may not achieve all of those qualities but you can get close to them. For many years I used an Olympus XA-3 camera, with a detachable A11 flash, which met most of the above requirements. I now have a Pentax Zoom-70 which meets even more of my requirements. (But I still miss my lovely little Olympus.) Camera choice is always a matter of compromise — sorting out which feature is more important than another.

There are, of course, problems with all cameras. Perhaps the greatest difficulty with a compact — in my experience, which may be aggravated by the fact that I wear glasses — is the viewfinder. Whereas the ground-glass screen of the SLR is truly WYSIWYG, the viewfinder on a compact is not.

If you tightly compose a picture using a compact with a zoom or long-focus lens, you can easily end up with partially decapitated bodies or incomplete buildings. You need to be very careful in allowing for the displaced view of the longer lenses.

Most compacts with longer-focus facilities have second picture-boundary 'frames' outlined in the viewfinder, for the changed lens. But 'in the heat of the moment' it is all too easy to overlook the displaced frame-lines and compose to the full extent of the wide-angle frame. Or to get the frame-size right but to miss the displacement of its view.

That problem apart, a compact with as many of the

features recommended above as possible, is an ideal camera for most writer-photographers. And for the more enthusiastic it is a very sensible everyday compliment to a more complex SLR.

The sophisticated SLR

The increased electronic sophistication and associated ease of use of the compact has inevitably had an effect on the SLR. You can now get a good quality SLR with many of the features of an up-market compact. And the SLR retains its WYSIWYG and lens interchange advantages.

For the more enthusiastic writer-photographer, let us list the characteristics of a good, inexpensive SLR and then those of the more sophisticated, easy-to-use SLR. And this will also interest the writer-photographer who perhaps wishes to 'graduate up' from a compact. First, the straightforward SLR.

For writer-photographer use, I believe that any SLR should have:

- lens interchangeability — and a range of available lenses; (and look for a range of lenses that includes a wide-angle/long-focus zoom.)
- a facility, on the ground-glass screen, for critical focussing — usually a slightly enlarged split circle wherein the user matches the alignment of verticals;
- a built-in exposure meter operating through the lens, which permits the exposure to be adjusted without removing the camera from the eye. (This is often by adjusting the lens aperture ring so as to align two pointers within the viewfinder.) The film

speed will have to be set — on the camera — by the user;

- shutter speeds varying from 1 to 1/1000 second, plus 'B' — for time exposures;
- a depth of field preview facility — because SLRs focus at full aperture, you need to see in advance the effect on the focussing of the automatic stopping down to correct aperture;
- a means of attaching and using flash — today, this almost goes without saying.

A variety of good solid SLRs which meet the above requirements can be had for around £120 to £150. Look particularly at the Russian and East German SLRs which are extremely good value for money. One of the Prakticas would probably be a sensible 'first proper camera', capable of producing just about any picture that an enthusiastic writer-photographer would wish to attempt.

With quite a bit more money available — and preferably a technical understanding such as this chapter has offered to the beginner — several more sophisticated cameras are available. These offer, in addition to the basics:

- automatic film loading, film speed setting (by DX coding) and automatic advance and rewind; (some auto-advance mechanisms can be as fast as a motor-drive — ideal for action photography.)
- automatic focussing — with a variety of suitable lenses — including the facility to 'hold' a pre-focussed setting; (this is used, for example, in action photography: you focus on a spot on the road and then pan with a car until it reaches the

pre-focussed spot; only then do you trigger the shutter release.)

- automatic — and programmed, to select the most suitable shutter speed/aperture setting — exposure metering and setting; (the best SLRs take several meter readings within the picture-boundary frame and then balance the exposure-setting accordingly. The user can also select a preferred aperture or a preferred shutter speed and the camera will adjust the setting to allow for this.)

- built-in flash with metering of the necessary amount of light required from it — and the ability to switch it off.

Again, there are a variety of high quality cameras that will meet all or most of the above requirements. They are very easy to use — as easy as a compact; but you have to pay for this ease. Around £300 is the current price for a camera complete with all the available 'bells and whistles'.

To summarise my advice to the aspiring writer-photographer then: a really good compact will probably suffice; if you want more, go for a good, solid, non-automatic SLR — and hold onto your compact, you can use both. If money is no particular object, a fully automatic SLR is a marvellous thing to have. But it is not *necessary*.

2

TAKING GOOD PICTURES

Once upon a time, a photographer was a man who draped a cloth over his head and peered into a large wooden box supported on a tripod. After some time, he came out from under the cloth and said, 'Watch the birdie.' Everyone then 'froze' for several seconds while the picture was taken. Often the photographer took another picture as a safety precaution. Sometimes, he used a flash: a large bulb that lit brightly — and briefly — went 'pop', and then had to be thrown away.

More recently — in my time even — a photographer would have to measure the light falling on the subject and adjust various knobs and dials on the camera before the picture could be taken. With experience though, the exposure could be judged for urgent photographic opportunities. And tripods became less common.

Today, most of the technical side of photography has been automated. The photographer CAN still make decisions on exposure, use of flash, etc. BUT HE/SHE DOESN'T NEED TO.

To produce photographs of excellent technical quality today, it is possible to do little more than just *point and shoot*. The rankest amateur can now produce good 'ordinary' pictures that will stand comparison with the work of most professional photographers. Given the will, *any* writer can become a writer-photographer.

The one remaining requirement of the photographer is 'an eye'. To take good 'ordinary' — saleable — photographs, you need to be able to *see* the picture. (For the moment, we will concentrate on *how* to picture the subject; the *choice* of subject is dealt with in Chapter 3.)

Common faults — and the cures

Let us first think about the commonest faults in amateur photographs. The worst of these are:

- a blurred picture — but with a sharp background
- a fuzzy picture — nothing sharp at all
- half of the picture obscured, the rest OK
- moving subject 'fuzzy' — with all else sharp
- 'headless wonders'
- unidentifiable tiny people
- pale and 'wishy-washy', or dark and gloomy, pictures
- reclining buildings, floors and people
- the photographer's shadow intruding into the picture.

Own up. Haven't you had at least some pictures that fit those descriptions?

The reasons for the above faults — and how to correct them – are basic to successful photography. They have nothing to do with difficult technicalities. They don't have much to do with having a good 'eye' for a picture, either. To correct them, you just need to take a little care.

In detail therefore, the common faults and their cures:

The blurred picture: The sharp background is the clue here. The camera has not been correctly focussed.

If the camera is a fixed-focus compact, then you have not paid attention to the camera instructions about how closely you may approach your subject. (These will often say something like, 'Everything from 10 feet to infinity is in focus.') Point your camera at something four or five feet away and the result will be blurred — but the background will be sharp.

If the camera is a compact with variable distance settings — perhaps a tiny picture of a mountain scene, a person from head to toe, and a head and shoulders only — then you have probably set the focus incorrectly or left the chosen setting from a previous picture.

If the camera is a 'proper' single-lens reflex and the picture is out of focus — you have probably 'grabbed' the shot without focussing. Or pressed the shutter release by accident. (Or your eyes need testing.)

If your camera is one of the highly sophisticated ones with auto-focus, there are two possibilities: either you fully pressed the shutter release a wee bit too quickly, before the auto-focussing process was complete, or there is a fault in the camera. And if the fault occurs only occasionally, it is more likely to be you than the camera.

To produce saleable pictures to accompany your

written work, they must be sharp. You must focus carefully and accurately. Or, you must accept the reasonable limitations of the camera's fixed focus.

The 'fuzzy-all-over' picture: This is almost certainly due to the camera moving whilst the picture was being taken. This is known as 'camera shake'.

(If just part of the picture — a moving car or a person — is fuzzy while the background is sharp, this is 'subject movement'. *See* below.)

Whatever your camera, you should always do your best to hold it steady. Don't try one-handed pictures, hold the camera securely with both hands; hug your elbows in to your sides and stand as firmly as possible. If taking pictures indoors, or elsewhere in poor light, look out for somewhere on which you can rest the camera. (Never neglect the possibility of pressing the camera against the side of a column; even though the camera is not actually supported, there is little chance of it then shaking.)

Another tip for holding the camera steady is to pull against its neck-strap. Some photographers even wind the strap around their elbow — much like a competitive marksman.

Of course, the 'final' answer to camera shake is to use a tripod. But this is often somewhat 'over the top' for a mere writer-photographer. Perhaps a less ostentatious alternative is to use a monopod: a single extendable 'leg' (effectively one leg of a tripod) which although it will not stop the camera swaying, will certainly stop it shaking.

One other reason for camera shake is the 'jabbed' shutter release. You should always *squeeze* the shutter release button into the rest of the camera; 'jabbing' at it inevitably causes the camera to move. 'Jabbing' like this may lead to camera shake; it may also cause the horizon to tilt. The two faults together make diagnosis simple.

(Without a tripod, it is sometimes possible to obviate camera movement by resting the camera on something firm — and using the self-timer release to take the picture. The camera cannot 'jab' its own release.)

If your camera is a single-lens reflex, with adjustable shutter speeds, then it is likely that an all-over-fuzzy picture is caused by too slow a shutter speed. (With a compact camera, shutter speeds are seldom adjustable.) My own practice is to use a minimum shutter speed of 1/125 seconds — until I need to vary this for some other reason. And when I have to reduce that speed I take care to find extra support, or hold the camera more firmly — with a wind-around strap, for instance.

As soon as you fit an alternative, usually longer, lens onto your reflex camera, you need an even faster shutter speed. A long lens considerably increases the likelihood of camera shake. With a longer than standard lens on my camera, I standardise on a 1/250 second shutter speed. Or support it better, preferably with a tripod.

And one last reason for a 'fuzzy-all-over' is the camera shake caused by vibration. If you try to photograph through a moving car, coach or train window, you should avoid pressing the camera to the glass. The glass will be vibrating, possibly without your noticing. But the camera will get the shakes.

The partially obscured picture: This, a fuzzy shapeless blob across part of the picture is always due to a finger, a strap, or half a camera case, partially obscuring the lens.

The cure for this fault is obvious: don't do it. And it will help to prevent the intrusive camera case if you dispose of the so-called 'ever-ready case' with its flopping flap. Either keep the camera 'naked' and hanging round your neck, ready for instant use — or keep it in a camera holdall.

The blur of movement: If you try to photograph a racing car, or an athlete — or even just a passer-by — you are liable to get trouble with movement blur. This is entirely due to the shutter speed being insufficient to 'freeze' the movement. (Of course, it is sometimes done deliberately in the more 'artistic' of photographs. But these are seldom the type of picture that a writer-photographer could reasonably submit with the average feature article.)

There are two possible solutions/cures for this problem: using a faster shutter speed or 'panning' the camera with the moving subject.

The shutter speed needed to freeze movement depends — understandably — on the speed of the movement, but also on the closeness of the subject to the camera. Without panning, and with the subject sufficiently close to the camera to more-or-less fill the frame, and moving directly across the screen, you will need:

- walker .. ..1/250 sec
- runner .. ..1/1000 sec
- cyclist.. .. ..1/2000 sec
- car (80 km/h) .. ..impossible

If the subject is further away — occupying perhaps no more than the middle third of the screen — or is just as close as before, but *moving diagonally towards* the camera, the above speeds can be halved. (That is, for example, 1/125 sec will suffice for a walker.) The 'distant' car can now be photographed with a 1/2000 sec exposure, and the 'diagonal' car with 1/1000 sec.

If you pan the camera though, a shutter speed of 1/125 sec will suffice in almost all cases. What then, is panning?

To pan the camera with a moving subject, you frame the subject in the viewfinder or on the screen some while before it reaches the point at which you intend to picture it — and on which you have already focussed. Then you follow the subject's movement in the viewfinder, moving the camera round as the subject approaches you. When the subject is just about at the required spot, *while continuing to move the camera and to follow the subject in the viewfinder*, the shutter is released. (You need to anticipate the arrival at 'the spot' to some extent — to allow for the time for the shutter to operate.)

The result of panning should be a sharply focussed and 'frozen' subject against a blurred background. The blur of the background undoubtedly increases the impact of the photograph; it enhances the 'feel' of movement. (The degree of blur in the background will of course depend on the subject's speed of movement — and hence the speed at which the camera has been panned.)

A word of warning though: although 1/125 sec may freeze the *overall* movement of, say, a cyclist, the legs the pedals or the wheel-spokes — or all three — may still be blurred; neither panning nor the 1/125 sec exposure will cope with the localised extra speed of these movements.

Headless wonders: A classic beginners' fault, due to

insufficient care in framing the picture in the viewfinder. Beginners seemingly ignore the framelines superimposed within the viewfinder and assume that everything that can be seen will be photographed.

This is particularly the case when the camera, usually a compact, has two lenses available — and the second, smaller, and often off-set, frame showing within the viewfinder is ignored. (I had several spoiled shots on the first roll using my new zoom-lenses compact.) Most often it is pure carelessness; it was so, in my case.

(Headless wonders can also, sometimes, be a result of a combination of over-tight framing and automatic film processing: automatic processing equipment — as used for 'happy snaps' — seldom prints the whole of any negative. This is not really the fault of the aspiring photographer, who will learn by experience.)

The 'cure' for pictorially decapitated in-laws (or whoever) is simple. Don't do it. Learn the limits — and quirks — of your viewfinder. Then leave a wee bit of 'slack' around the subject. (But not too much slack: *see* below.)

Midgetitis: One of the worst faults of just about every beginner is to take pictures of tiny people. This is because most beginners photograph subjects from too far away. 'Aunt Mabel is that person over there in the background, just beside that bush.' If the picture is supposed to be of Aunt Mabel, why was the photographer not much — MUCH — closer to her? Aunt Mabel should just about fill the frame — even if she isn't overweight.

There is a lot more to be said about filling the picture with its subject — but that comes later in this chapter.

For now, the cure for midgetitis — tiny unidentifiable people in the far background of your pictures — is to get closer. So long as you avoid decapitation (and distortion — *see* below), it is almost impossible to be too close to a picture's subject. (But be careful though: you need to know what the subject really is.)

Pale or gloomy pictures: Inevitably, pale, washed-out pictures are the result of over-exposure; similarly, dark, gloom-laden pictures result from under-exposure. There can be several reasons for this.

You may be pointing the camera towards a bright light — into the sun or, indoors, towards a window; you may have set the film speed wrongly on the camera; or you may be using the flash at too close a distance. Any one of those faults will lead to an over-exposed, that is, a washed out, picture.

The dull, gloomy pictures can be the result of the camera having been fooled by a bright light in part of the picture — and therefore under-exposing the rest. Or maybe you have tried to take a flash photograph from too far away. The light from the built-in flash will only light up relatively close subjects. Or, as with washed-out over-exposure, a gloomy under-exposed picture can result from having set the incorrect film speed on the camera.

With any camera without auto-exposure, either washed-out or gloomy pictures could simply mean that you set the exposure incorrectly.

The cure for wrongly-exposed pictures is to expose them correctly. Take particular care when loading film into your camera that the film speed is correctly set. (If you always use one type of film, this will not be a problem — until the one occasion when you load a different film.)

The modern DX films and cameras preclude incorrect film-speed setting; the camera 'reads' the film speed from the film cartridge as it is loaded. (There are sets of contact points within the camera and carefully-positioned coded areas on the cartridge.) You merely have to ensure that you only buy film marked 'DX'.

Camera settings aside, pay attention to the range of distances at which your built-in flash is effective. And stay within the range.

When not using flash, pay attention to the make-up of your picture — avoid pointing the camera *directly* into a light. You can sometimes change your viewpoint so that the actual light source is obscured — and a back-lit subject can then often be most effective.

Falling-over subjects: You are photographing a building from the far side of the road; you can't quite get the top in; you point the camera up a little to include the whole. When the prints come back from processing, the building somehow looks as though it is falling over — towards you. This is a common fault.

Other pictures of buildings show them falling over sideways. This is a different fault: you are not framing the picture properly — OR, as you release the shutter, you are tipping the camera sideways a little.

To photograph buildings well, the camera must — but must — be held level; it must not be tipped up. Alternative solutions are:

● move further back (and trim off the resultant excessive foreground when printing),
● change your position so that you are photographing from higher up the building, or
● use a wide- (or wider-) angle lens.

The cure for buildings that tip sideways is simple. You must learn to *squeeze*, rather than stab at, the shutter release. (Similarly, a soldier has to learn to squeeze, rather than pull, the trigger of a gun; pulled triggers miss targets.)

Intrusive shadows: Photographing with the sun behind you, for 'a good, well-lit picture', your own shadow stretches far ahead of you — and can dominate the foreground of the picture. Watch out for it.

The cure for this is to change your viewpoint so that your shadow moves 'out of frame'. It might, alternatively, be a good idea to take the picture back-lit, with fill-in flash.

Fault-stoppers

It is useful to summarise the dos and don'ts that we have covered in the above 'cures'. They won't ensure that your pictures are all 'good 'uns' — but they will help to ensure that the pictures you do take will be worth looking at. 'Better pictures' comes next.

So . . . 'fault-stoppers':

- focus carefully (on the subject) — or work within the range at which your camera is sharply focussed;
- use a fast (-ish) shutter speed whenever possible, and always hold your camera steady, taking every opportunity to support it;
- discard your camera case — and watch out for stray straps or fingers obscuring the lens;
- if you need to photograph a moving subject, pan the camera — and use the fastest possible shutter speed;
- get to know the peculiarities of your viewfinder and frame your pictures accordingly;

- get close to your subject — then get closer still;
- avoid bright lights facing into the camera, work within correct flash range, and ensure the film speed is correctly set;
- hold your camera level and gently *squeeze* the shutter release;
- *kill* your own intrusive shadow — by shifting viewpoint.

Picture content

Follow the above 'rules' and your pictures will immediately be better — much better — than the average. They will at least be worth looking at. Now let's see how we can improve the quality of the picture content.

Ways in which you can make better-looking, more attractive, pictures include:

- good composition
- getting close
- good contrast (remember, you're taking black and white pictures)
- making the picture 'stand out' from its background.

And really, each of these 'ways' is inter-related with the others; and they are all to do with composition.

Before we look in detail at these ways of improving the quality of your pictures, there is one prior fundamental consideration.

You need to determine the subject of your picture.

'Don't be daft,' I hear you say. 'Of course I know what the picture is going to be of.' Maybe. But if you do indeed know the subject — why does the picture not concentrate on it? Why can I, the viewer, not be sure what the picture is all about?

You may think, initially, that your subject is, say, the village church. What you have *written about* though, may be the carvings on the church door, or the weather-vane atop the spire, or the fact that the whole building is leaning over. The real subject of your picture should perhaps be the carvings, the weather-vane or 'the lean'. And a photograph that concentrates on these will probably be a better one. It will almost certainly be more saleable.

The message is, narrow your subject down — and then photograph that.

Of course, there will often still be a need for a picture of the whole church — but less often than it is photographed. Think hard — what does the picture need to show? When you have decided that, go out and photograph it. The resultant picture will be better — as an article-writer's picture — than many. It will probably be just what the editor wants.

Composing the picture

Now, some thoughts on simple composition. That may be a frightening word — but it's a relatively simple idea. The composition of a picture is no more than the judicious — attractive — placing of the parts of the picture within the overall frame. And the easiest way of conveying the basic concepts of composition is probably in an extended list.

Figure 2.1 illustrates three classic faults and a handful of recommended ways of achieving 'good' composition.

To improve the formal composition of your pictures:

44

- Locate important pictorial elements at the one-third points.

  Imagine that the top, bottom and each side of your picture frame is divided into three; draw (imaginary) lines from top to bottom and from side to side, linking up the one-third points, effectively dividing the whole picture up into nine equal rectangles. The four points at which the dividing lines intersect are 'the one-third points' of the picture — and it is on these points that the viewer's attention is most likely to concentrate.

- Watch your horizon — make sure that you don't cut your picture in two.

  In landscape particularly, but to a lesser extent in almost any picture, it is important to think about horizontal lines. Any horizontal line, particularly an unbroken one, will tend to divide the picture in two. And two equal halves are very boring. (The same principles apply to a vertical line dividing the picture in two. But such lines are less common.)

  As a general rule, therefore, arrange your picture so that the horizon is somewhere near the quarter or one-third points. (Again, the importance of the one-third points.) And the horizon does not always have to be near the top of a picture; it can — with much impact — sometimes be better near the bottom. A low horizon enhances the strength of, for instance, a nicely clouded sky.

  Occasionally too, for real impact, try losing the horizon altogether; do this by tilting the camera right up, or right down.

- Emphasise — and use – the diagonals.

  If some part of the picture can follow the diagonal line linking either pair of opposite corners, this will give a strength and cohesiveness to the

Fig. 2.1

A few of the classic photographic faults – and some examples of how to achieve "good" composition.

1   A bad case of "midgetitis" – the subjects of the picture are far too far away from the photographer. Cure: get closer.

2   An example of headless wonders – which may have been the result of ignoring the more limiting viewfinder frame. Cure: pay attention to viewfinder. More important, the picture cries out to be a vertical one – turn the camera on its side and get both in, from head to boring toe. Better still, get closer, as in 3.

3   A good example of how to photograph a couple. The photographer has approached close and because of the relative heights of the subjects, has achieved a good near-diagonal composition. And it is nicely off-centre.

4   The action is moving into the picture. The viewer's attention is nicely retained. It is well composed too – the notional future path of the ball is not unlike a winding stream, and follows the diagonal too.

5 Here, the back and side of a person's head in the foreground, dominates the whole composition, making a comparatively "flat" landscape much more interesting.

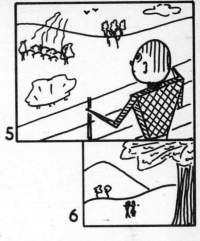

6 No person in the foreground, but the tree not only dominates the foreground but also acts as a partial frame to the picture. And notice how people are included in the picture – to give it "human appeal".

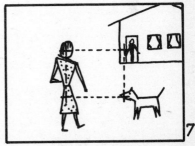

7 The "one-third points" are here shown clearly – and illustrate how strong the resultant composition is.

8 The classic "intrusive background" fault. Not only does the tree sprout from the person's head but the bricks of the wall behind do not offer any contrast with the subject. But at least it's a vertical picture. Cure: move the subject (or the wall).

9 A good example of choice of background. Not only does the well-lit musician stand out clearly against the dark background but its very darkness suggests an atmosphere very appropriate for a jazz musician.

design. Think of a portrait with the face on a slant such that a line through forehead, nose and mouth follows the diagonal; this will often be more impressive than a completely upright portrait.

Use the diagonals too for a path or stream winding its way through a picture. It will also help, if the winding path or stream actually gets somewhere — near to a one-third point — within the picture. Take care to ensure that the winding diagonal does not lead the eye out of the picture.

• Attract attention to within the picture — don't actively encourage viewers to look beyond the frame.

If you photograph a person looking at something outside the frame of the picture, the viewer will want to see what this is. The viewer's interest will be drawn outside the frame. Conversely, if the picture shows someone looking at something which is itself within the picture-frame, so too will the viewer's attention be directed.

The same principles apply to activities. If, for instance, a ball is being kicked, or a car driven, out of the frame, the viewer's interest goes with it. Drive the car and kick the ball *into the picture*. Always try to leave more space in front of a movement than behind the activator/mover.

Another way of encouraging the eye to remain within the bounds of the picture is to draw the eye around and inwards. You can do this by locating significant items within the picture around an imaginary inward-looking spiral; the eye follows the spiral.

An S-shaped arrangement of pictorial elements will also draw the eye upwards and inwards. This

48

is particularly so, if the lower half of the S starts with a strong foreground object.

- Look for and emphasise any patterns that form, or can be found, within your picture.

Rows of chairs receding into the background are a common pattern; the lines left on a sandy shore by the receding tide form a strong pattern; so too does strong side-light falling on a clap-board fence or building face. Even the regular geometric pattern of paving slabs can suggest a chessboard-like approach to a more distant figure or activity.

Patterns can often be emphasised by changing the camera position: by getting down low, near the ground, or by finding a higher viewpoint — by standing on a wall perhaps. (As long as you are not photographing specific buildings, ie, in an architectural context, it doesn't matter that you occasionally tilt the camera. Particularly if you tilt it *positively* — for dramatic effect.)

- Watch for, and use, strong shadows — particularly those that come from side-lighting. Remember, you will be photographing almost exclusively in black and white. You *need* the contrasts of light and shade.

It pays to go out searching for illustrations for your articles in the early (-ish) morning, or late afternoon. At those times, the sun is lower in the sky and casts its light more sideways; and side-lighting means stronger, more dramatic shadows.

- Dominate the foreground.

As we have already mentioned, many of the suggestions about composition inter-relate with others. And this is particularly the case with the advice to dominate the foreground. A strong foreground element can be the start of a sweeping Scurve or the inward look or the travel of an activity within the frame. It is also, of course, particularly relevant to the important concept, not yet elaborated on, of getting in close to the subject. (*See* below.)

The concept of foreground domination is very important in the photographing of landscapes. A landscape that 'looks good' to the naked eye will seldom make a strong photograph. The eye automatically concentrates selectively on elements within the scene it is looking at; the camera pictures the whole scene — it cannot exercise selectivity.

So the photographer must provide the interest; and this is most easily done by adding a foreground figure looking — selectively — at the scene. Once again, the viewer's eye is drawn along the lines suggested by the foreground figure.

The foreground interest in a landscape does not have to be a person looking at the scene. It could equally well be an animal: but show the animal's head, looking into the picture . . . not the back end of the animal. (That's seldom attractive.)

Many of the same advantages can be derived from an inanimate object in the foreground. A tree can effectively frame part of the picture, offering both foreground interest and, at the same time, drawing the eye round, spiralling inwards from the trunk and foliage. The lychgate approach to a picturesque village church can provide a similar, framing, benefit. Always watch out for natural frames and relevant foreground material.

- Fit the background to the picture — and vice versa.

The subject of a picture should stand out from its background. If it merges with the background, it disappears. And remember again, while the colouring of the subject may provide real-life differentiation, this may well disappear in black and white.

Everyone knows to avoid the tree growing out of Aunt Mabel's head — but too many of us forget it, in *the heat* of photographic enthusiasm. (Yes, I have my failures too.) But there is more to think about than just the tree-topped head. An outdoor portrait may usefully be set against a clear sky; but if the picture is of say, a jazz musician, the sky would be a highly inappropriate backdrop. (The traditional 'image' of a jazz musician would have them seldom seeing the light of day.)

At a general, more mundane, level: always seek a light-coloured, clutter-free background for a dark subject and a darker, equally un-fussy background for a light-coloured subject. It makes sense.

● Fill the viewfinder frame with the picture — ie, get in close.

If you are photographing an object — a piece of jade, a wooden carving, a street light — for its own sake, the only thought you should give to composition is to centre the subject. Well, just a wee bit off the centre perhaps. But don't bother to look too hard for diagonals or one-third points; just photograph it. Get in close, picture it big, and avoid waste space around it.

The readers of your article want to see what you are referring to in the text. They are not looking for an artistic representation.

If you are photographing a person, the readers will usually want to see their face. Not their feet.

Again, get in close. (But watch out for photographic distortion; use a long-focus lens to fill the frame.) But don't merely centre a head; leave somewhere for the subject to look — frame it slightly off-centre. Maybe — but be careful about when you do this — even tilt the head to pick up a diagonal. Notice too how I worded the advice at the head of this item. I said, '. . . fill the frame *with the picture.*' I did not say, 'with the subject'. In some cases, you will want to make *the picture* more than just the subject. Then, you will want to apply many of the concepts of composition that we have outlined above. The important thing is to avoid including extraneous elements.

- Include people — or indicators of people (eg, motorcars) — in pictures wherever possible. Buildings or empty landscapes devoid of humanity can be dull — and are often unsaleable.

Even if you are not using a person to dominate the foreground of a picture — perhaps because the composition is better with a framing tree — it is still desirable to have a person somewhere in view. People give *scale* to a picture.

A warning though. Because you should be able to continue selling the same picture for many years, beware extremes of fashion. A view including a man wearing flared trousers would look very dated today.

- Pictures can be upright; they don't all have to be horizontal.

One of the hallmarks of the amateur photographer is that all his/her photographs are horizontal — because that's the way the camera is easiest to hold. (Similarly, when using a 'half-frame' 35 mm camera, where the 'comfortable-holding' format is vertical, amateur photographers take mainly vertical pictures.) But some pictures *demand* a vertical format. Think of a (painted' portrait: nine times out of ten it will be an upright picture — because that is the 'natural' format for an upright subject. Yet photographers frequently struggle to portray a person — or a church and its spire — within the horizontal format imposed by their cameras.

Be different. Be professional. Turn the camera on its side and take a vertical picture of a vertical subject.

(As we shall see, in the next chapter, editors welcome a choice — particularly including vertical pictures.)

Viewpoint

In the above section we have looked at how a picture should be composed; what the end result should look like. 'That's all very well,' I hear you say. 'But I can't move that building in order to improve the composition of my photograph.' Nor are such Herculean tasks necessary.

You may not physically be able to move the elements which make up your picture — but you can certainly move the camera. You can move the camera up, down, sideways, or any combination of these. You can come closer — or you can move further away. And as you change the camera's viewpoint, so too do you re-arrange the disposition — *in the viewfinder* — of the features you are photographing.

Some of the effects that come from changing the viewpoint, can also be obtained by changing the camera lens. Move back and pull the picture closer again with a long-focus lens; or vice versa, with a wide-angle lens. And changing both the lens and the viewpoint direction can create an even more dramatic composition. Experiment. Take more than one picture too.

Similarly, you may not wish, or it may not be possible, to change the viewpoint; but you may still be able to vary the lighting. A subject lit from directly behind the camera will look flat and uninteresting; early in the morning or late in the afternoon, the side-light may be such that the subject creates dramatic shadows. The shadows themselves can make an effective composition. (And a back-lit subject can be even more dramatic — as long as the exposure is 'right', whatever that may mean.)

Whatever you do, however you juggle the elements in your picture-frame or look for different, more dramatic lighting, you will sometimes be stuck with a dull picture. In such cases, try photographing just a part of the whole. Part of a building can often look more attractive, when photographed, than the whole.

As ever, it pays to experiment. Always take more than one photograph of each potential picture. Vary the viewpoint, vary the lens, vary the lighting.

3

SALEABLE PICTURES

If you have paid attention to the recommendations in the previous chapters, you will find that now, more often than not, you are producing acceptable pictures. The only thing left is to take *the right pictures*.

To the writer-photographer, *the right pictures* are those that editors buy. They are pictures that enhance the saleability of your feature articles.

So, what sort of pictures do editors want?

To answer that question, all you need do is look at the pictures that the same editors are currently using. That is, study the pictures that illustrate the articles in the magazine to which you intend to sell.

A look at one market

Let us study a recent issue of *The Lady* — which is one of the *better* British markets for unsolicited illustrated feature articles. (Better, at least, in the sense that *The Lady* buys more unsolicited features each year than most other publications.) And the issue at which we shall look just happens to include an illustrated article of my own — which is reproduced at Figure 3.1, and to which we shall refer again.

The first thing to note is that, with the exception of the cover photograph, the entire magazine is illustrated in black and white. There are no colour photographs at all.

The first three-and-a-bit editorial pages (as opposed to the preceding twenty-two pages of, mainly small, advertisements) of the magazine are taken up with largely staff-written news and comment. ('Largely' because there is also usually a contributed 'Viewpoint' feature within this section.) These pages include nine photographs, all with some news content. All are reasonably topical; most are probably provided by press photographs or agencies.

The next one-and-two-thirds pages are occupied by my own feature 'In Praise of Dragons'. (Fig. 3.1) This is illustrated with four photographs, all upright, all of dragons; three are statues, the fourth is a dressed-up Morris dancer — being fed by my son. The three 'statue' dragons all stand out well in dark detail against a pale background. We will come back to that article again, later.

The next two pages of the magazine are a two-page spread about fishing for cockles in Leigh-on-Sea. The article is entitled 'Alive, Oh!' — of course. There are four excellent photographs, three upright, one horizontal (hereafter referred to as landscape).

One of the pictures is of a young boy jumping happily onto a pile of cockle-shells; two show fishermen carrying and delivering baskets of cockles; the third, the landscape one, shows a cockle boat. In each, there is someone doing something — even on the cockle boat.

The pictures were taken by someone other than the writer of the article. Both writer and photographer were credited.

The next two-page spread is an author-illustrated article about the town of Newark, entitled 'For the Sake of Peaches and New Cider'. (This is a reference to King John, who died of a surfeit of such refreshments in 1216.) The feature is illustrated with three photographs, all landscape: a view of the castle from across the river; a picture of a tiny sixteenth-century Bede House chapel; and a picture of some small, attractive, timbered shops in the town centre.

There is not a person in sight in any of the pictures, but one — of the Bede House — has evidence of human life in the shape of a couple of parked cars. The pictures are much like you would find on picture postcards of the town's attractions.

The next two pages are devoted to the island of Lanzarote. A feature entitled 'Land of the Fire Mountains' includes five photographs by the author: three are landscape and two are upright.

The three landscape pictures are, to me, very ordinary — distant scenes with no strong centre of interest. (They would not be out of place in a beginner's holiday snap-shot album.) The two upright pictures are rather better: one is a portrait of a camel; the other, a tall cactus pictured alongside a town centre streetlight. The pictures were presumably used in the absence of anything better. In this case, I would think that the article carried — ie, helped to sell — the pictures, rather than the more usual reverse.

Next comes a two-page spread about a particularly interesting Paris cemetery. Bob Collins contributes a

Gordon Wells
writes

In
Praise
of
Dragons

*pictures
by the
author*

right: The fine dragon
supporting the Cadiz cannon
at Horseguards' Parade
in London.
below: The City of London
dragon, outside the
Law Courts.

To CASTIGATE a female disciplinarian or a boarding-house landlady by referring to her as an 'old dragon' is almost certainly unfair – on both the lady and the dragon. But it is all part of our tradition.

To the English, the dragon is supposedly bad news. After all, our patron saint owes his reputation to having killed one. The battle between St George and the dragon took place probably in the sixth century, on Dragon Hill, near Uffington in Oxfordshire – or was it at Brinsop, near Hereford? – and presumably on 23 April.

Well, not really. George was a Turkish officer in the Roman army of the early fourth century, and he never visited England at all. And it was not until 1350 that King Edward III founded the Order of the Garter and made George the patron saint of England.

He has the same honoured status in Russia too. St George is the patron saint of the Russian state of Georgia – but that's not where its name comes from – and again is venerated for killing a dragon. (In Russia recently I picked up a painted tile depicting a glamorous Georgii killing the Russian dragon.) The ubiquitous George was also at one time the patron saint of Genoa.

The tales of George's victory over the dragon were probably inspired by medieval religious symbolism. The dragon represented the forces of evil vanquished by the church. One story of George and 'his' dragon was told by Edmund Spenser in his poem *The Faerie Queene*; the story was also told in William Caxton's 1483 English edition of *The Golden Legend*.

A lesser-known dragon saga is the tale of the Lambton Worm, first set down in the nineteenth century. The Worm was a dragon which was so long that it curled itself three times around Worm Hill – at Fatfield, south of Newcastle – and terrorized the neighbourhood. It was finally cut in two and

Fig. 3.1

A reproduction of the author's "In Praise of Dragons" as used in The
Lady. *Notice the upright/landscape photographs.*

above: Feeding the Chanctonbury Morris men's dragon. *right:* The Beijing dragon, in its chicken-wire armour.

led by young Sir John Lambton; nsequently the whole Lambton family s cursed.

An older folk tale, first recorded in the enteenth century, tells – in earthy detail – a cunning Yorkshire knight's duel with other dragon. The knight, called More of ore Hall, fought the Dragon of Wantley, ar Rotherham, for 'two days and a night' thout either side being wounded. Finally, ore 'came like a lout' and slew the dragon th a particularly well-aimed kick at posterior.

ARADOXICALLY, while the dragon was vilified by church and story-tellers alike, it s also a popular symbol of strength and our. Many a Roman legionary marched neath an SPQR banner topped with a gon. The Vikings, who preyed on anyone lish enough to live too near the sea, velled in longboats adorned with dragons. eed, Norse mythology also has a dragon ing at the roots of the Tree of Life.

But we need not even leave these British es to find the dragon being accorded pect. The symbol of Wales is the Red agon. (A white dragon, representing the xons, fought with a red dragon, resenting the Welsh, in an underground e at Caernarvon; the white dragon lost. er since, the Welsh have looked to the red gon for support against the Anglo-Saxons.) d King Arthur's father, Uther Pendragon, aid to have had two green dragons, back to k, in his coat of arms, and had a gold gori 'to carry about with him in the wars'. To this day, dragons are all about us. A ely sculpted dragon supports the City of ndon shield on the top of the Temple Bar morial (outside the Law Courts, where et Street meets the Strand). Another fine

dragon supports the cannon of the Cadiz Memorial on Horseguards' Parade – a monument erected to commemorate the relief of Cadiz by Wellington and the British army in 1812.

In Brighton too, 'London-by-the-sea', there are dragons. They are rather less grand than the London ones, though. Stand outside Boots in North Street, near Brighton's Clock Tower, and look at the roofs on the opposite side of the road. There, sitting menacingly on the gable, waiting for a princess, is Brighton's finest dragon.

The Brighton dragon (and there are others elsewhere in the town) is a terracotta gable finial built into the roof around the turn of the century. Many houses then were finished off with 'claw and ball' finials; the more affluent house-buyers could choose more ornate designs. And the dragon was the most expensive of all the designs – at £1·40 in 1906.

LIVE DRAGONS are part of our British pageantry too. In Norwich the Snap Dragon still appears regularly, maintaining a tradition which goes back in an unbroken sequence to 1408. And the Sussex-based Chanctonbury Morris Men include a friendly dragon in their group, to the delight of their audiences.

More recently, the Chinese have brought their traditional lion and dragon dances to the streets of the larger British cities at Chinese New Year. The Chinese dragon is a long

snake-like creature made up of a dozen or more young men, its head usually operated by a two-man team. To the Chinese, the dragon has always been a symbol of good. The particularly lucky Imperial Dragon, recognizable by its five claws ('ordinary' dragons have only four claws), guarded not only the Emperor but also the 'flaming pearl', the sun.

Most Chinese dragons live in the sky, among the clouds. In the Forbidden City within Beijing – now open to tourists – there is a stone ramp up which the Emperor was carried; the ramp is covered with carvings of dragons sitting among carved clouds, guarding the Imperial person.

Like Brighton's gable finials, dragons protect the roofs of Chinese temples. Carved dragons march proudly along many a roof-line. While the evil European dragon lurks on the ground, it always has wings, whereas the good Chinese dragon, which lives in the clouds, is always wingless.

The Chinese belief in the luck-potential of their dragons causes problems now that ordinary people have access to the Imperial palaces. It is Chinese custom to touch a statue or carving for luck. And if a thousand million Chinese all touch the beautiful bronze dragon in the Summer Palace at Beijing for luck, it will soon wear away. So the dragon has to be shrouded in chicken-wire, to protect it.

St George was never needed in China. It is the dragon who needs protection there. ◌

thousand words and three striking photographs for 'Underground in Paris'. The three illustrations, two upright, one landscape, are all of gravestone sculptings — a striking bronze of a journalist, a bust of an elderly peasant-woman, and the grave of songbird Edith Piaf. The photographs are excellent and the text well-researched and interesting; the whole feature was clearly a welcome 'package' arriving on the editorial desk.

The next eight pages of *The Lady* are taken up with staff-written, or 'regular', columns on fashion, shopping, nature study/gardening etc. Then there is a page of advertisements.

This is followed by a single-page contributed article about the South Wales island of Skomer and its seabird colony. The thousand-word article is illustrated by a single, landscape, picture — by the author — of a herring gull. Someone, probably on the editorial staff, has blanked out the background of the photograph; in this way, it comes across with considerable impact. It also suggests that the original photograph had a distracting, over-fussy, background.

There are then three-and-a-half pages of staff-written features on cooking, and 'house and home' matters. Slipped in amongst these pages is a short, five hundred-word article about a Hong Kong street market — without illustrations. (A great pictorial opportunity missed.)

The editorial pages of this issue of *The Lady* are then finished off with five pages largely devoid of illustrations. (The only illustration is an historic line drawing reproduced with permission from the British Museum.) In all, the five pages include seven articles — at least two of which could have been much enhanced by a few photographs.

The final dozen-and-a-half pages are full of advertisements.

Summarising the contribution of the writer-photographer to this issue there are five illustrated articles, four filling double-page spreads. The average number of illustrations per article is just over three — rising to four if we exclude the article with just the single picture. Of the sixteen photographs, seven are upright and nine landscape — near enough half and half. (And as a matter of interest, of the nine 'news' pictures on the opening pages, five are upright; again, roughly half.)

The other interesting point is that six of the sixteen photographs are of statues or the like.

(The great merit of a statue is that it doesn't mind waiting while you sort out the best photographic 'angle'; and if you get it wrong, you can often go back and re-photograph it. Although I don't think I could justify the return fare to Beijing merely to re-photograph the wire-meshed dragon, should I have messed that one up.)

Remember: you should make a market study, much like the above, of any magazine for which you intend to contribute. Time spent on market study is NEVER wasted.

The dragon pictures

A more detailed look now, at the illustrations to my article about dragons (Figure 3.1). There is quite a lot to learn from these pictures.

In some ways the best picture in the set is that of my son feeding the Morris dancer dragon. It has the main interest — the dragon — but it also has a child in the picture; even better, the child is doing something, not just ogling the camera. It is the sort of picture that viewers can 'relate to'; everyone knows a young child who could be the one in the picture; it generates an almost certain, 'Oooh, isn't that cute?' response.

That child has now been married for several years; the picture was taken more than twenty years ago. It has sold several times, to different magazines; it is timeless; it will surely sell again. The child's clothes are not date-related; the dragon is 'dressed up' and could look the same this year as it did then; the cars in the background are sufficiently out of focus that their vintage is not obvious.

The picture of the Law Courts dragon has also sold before, and will sell again. It is a straightforward 'record' shot and has the advantage of standing out against the sky background. I chose the viewpoint carefully for just that reason.

The 'wire-mesh' dragon in Beijing has also been published before, and I expect to sell it several times more. It has two 'pluses': it's a nice big, 'interesting' dragon; and it is unusual in that you don't see many dragons wrapped up in protective chicken-wire.

I had to grab that picture in a hurry (the rest of our 'package' group was leaving and my wife was chivvying me along); given more time I would have found a better viewpoint. (Or at least another one.) A straight side or frontal view was difficult because of a fussy and crowded background. And there were too many people around. Ideally, I would have liked ten or a dozen pictures from which to choose.

The Cadiz canon dragon photograph is a new one. I had walked past it on many occasions, promising to bring my camera to town the next bright day — and kept forgetting. Finally, I got the picture. (I now have seven shots of this dragon; this one is probably the best. There is plenty of detail in the sculpting.)

In the package of photographs that I submitted with the manuscript to *The Lady*, there were other dragon pictures. In all, I submitted six photographs: the two that weren't used were one of the 'Brighton dragon' — a 'gable finial' made of terracotta and sitting on a town centre rooftop, which has sold several times already; and one of some wingless Chinese dragons guarding a pagoda roof-ridge — which has sold just once before.

Importance of sets

The dragon photographs sold as a package of words and pictures. The article might have sold without the illustrations — but it had MUCH more chance with them. Just one dragon picture MIGHT have been enough — but a *set* of several dragon pictures is much more saleable. And that's the important point. Pictures sell best *in sets*.

I have been collecting pictures of dragons for many years now. The pictures keep on selling — as do the articles they accompany. (And of course, in order to write the articles, I have had to research and collect factual material about the dragons too. But that's the writing side of the writer-photographer's business.)

Inevitably, I do not collect photographs only of dragons. Over the years I have collected *sets* of photographs of other things about which I intend to write.

I find the history of street lighting most interesting. And it is a subject that has not been done to death. I have therefore taken many photographs of unusual street lights — gas lanterns, ornate columns, ugly lanterns, and so on. And I have sold more than one illustrated article featuring these pictures. Figure 3.2 is

In 1805, the financier Mr F A Winsor founded the National Light and Heat Company, later to become the Gas Light and Coke Company. Something of a charlatan, he did much however to publicise the merits of gas lighting.

Winsor himself set up a row of triple lantern gas lights along Pall Mall. Ostensibly, this was to honour the king's birthday; but of course it was also an excellent advertisement. Four years later Pall Mall was permanently lit by gas.

Almost inevitably, there were those who condemned the new lights as 'profane and contrary to God's law'. Despite this criticism though,

> 'The task of maintaining and caring for these lights was made the responsibility of the Commissioners of ... Sewers!'

thousands of gas street lights were soon installed throughout London. (Paris lagged behind - the Parisians did not get gas street lights until 1818).

These early gas lights flickered and spluttered as the jets clogged up, the illumination was poor and changed colour - but the streets were lit. Many dastardly crimes were undoubtedly prevented. And certainly in central London, as Byron said of Brussels, ' ... bright the lamps shone o'er fair women and brave men.'

Soon however, a competitor arrived to contest with gas the right to light the streets. The first electric lamp was installed in the street outside the Gaiety Theatre, in 1877. And as with gas lighting, this new light caught the public's fancy. In 1881 electric lights were set up, on 80-feet-high lamp posts, outside the Bank of England, in the City.

Mantle

Possibly the competition of electric lighting spurred the development of

efficient. Gas could now compete on equal terms with the best that electricity could offer.

Gas street lights were quickly converted to use the incandescent mantle. The number of electric lights increased - but slowly. Gas held its own, comfortably, until the 1930s. A few gas lights remain to this day - but now they are merely picturesque anachronisms.

The lanterns, and the supporting columns, of these street lights are often fine examples of ornate Victorian design. Double and triple lanterns on leaf-embellished arms surmount tall fluted columns, guarded at the base by entwined fish and the like. Some lanterns are topped by crowns, others by crosses; some, out of sight, just seem to stop.

Squeezed

Not only were the gas-fired street lights attractive with their cheerful yellowish light and their pleasantly-designed lanterns and standards, but also they maintained the need for the picturesque lamplighter. With his long pole, he appeared regularly at dusk to light the lamps.

The pole, a tube, had a small oil lamp alight at the top and a rubber bulb at the bottom containing methylated spirits. As the bulb was squeezed it forced methylated spirits up the tube and past the oil lamp. There, it was ignited, producing a jet of flame which lit the gas mantle. Alas, other than in the Middle Temple, where a few gas lights remain to this day the lamplighter is no more.

Gas lights gradually gave way to the greater efficiency of electricity. Little by little, the ornate lanterns were converted to accept electric lights and many are still with us.

Electric street lighting is now

Decorative - and decorated - street lights along the Promenade at Worthing.

Fig. 3.2

A reproduction of the author's illustrated feature article on street lighting, as used in Christian Herald.

subject

AS WE DRIVE along our brightly-lit streets, it is worth recalling that it was not always so. Yet street lighting has a very long history.

In the third century, the streets of Rome were lit by lanterns hanging at the doors of all important buildings. The Greek philosopher Libanius reported that there was a quite extensive street lighting system in Antioch, about a hundred years later. The first record of organised street lighting in London though, is in the early 15th century.

In 1415 the householders of London were ordered to display a lighted lantern each winter evening at their street door. This order had only a limited effect. Few householders could afford the cost of it and certainly some who could, ignored the instructions.

By the 17th century though, the need for more effective street lighting was recognised, at least by the cities. Its main purpose was to reduce the burgeoning crime rate rather than to speed the traveller on his way. In 1657 the Aldermen of London were authorised to provide lights at public expense where householders could not be called upon to do so.

'Link boy'

Ten years later, the Paris police were insisting that their streets should be lit by lanterns at first floor level. Other European cities were also beginning to light their streets at about this same time: The Hague in 1618, Amsterdam in 1669, and Hamburg in 1675. However, it was not until 1736 that the first really comprehensive system of public street lighting came to London.

Once started, London's authorities made up for lost time. Within months there were 5,000 lights

operating in the city - and in two more years the number had risen to 15,000. The lights were provided 'at a distance of 30 yards from each other on each side of the greater streets and 35 yards in the lesser streets.'

The task of maintaining and caring for these lights was made the responsibility of the Commissioners of - no, not Roads or Lights - but Sewers! The lighting was not up to present-day standards. Just as today we drive with our lights on even in lit streets, in these early days a 'link boy', bearing a torch, walked in front of the sedan chairs, to light the way.

These early street lights were all oil-burning. But then came gas.

Charlatan

In 1765 a Mr Spedding succeeded in lighting his mine office with coal

gas. This was at Lord Lonsdale's coal mine, near Whitehaven. Mr Spedding suggested lighting the streets of Whitehaven with gas lamps - but the local magistrates refused his offer. There was then a 40-year delay before the first streets were lit by gas.

A less-than-elegant conversion of a gas light to electricity.

longer the incandescent bulbs of the early days, but highly efficient bulbs filled with sodium vapour. The light itself may be less attractive than the flicker of gas, but it is much brighter. The new lanterns and standards too, are clinical and efficient rather than picturesque. But the way is now much better lit.

Carl von Welsbach's invention of the incandescent mantle - a small impregnated silk or cotton bag which glowed brilliantly when heated - saved the gas street light from early extinction. Gas now heated the glowing mantle rather than shed light from its own flame. This new method was much more

Late 19th century triple lanterns in Trafalgar Square.

Lighting in The Lanes in Brighton - all converted to electricity, and some for advertising purposes.

A gas-fired street light that was still in use, not far from Piccadilly Circus in London, in the late 1960s.

Christian Herald, July 21, 1984

a reproduction of one such feature article. It appeared in *Christian Herald* which, sadly, is no longer a market for such general-interest illustrated features.

Another of my interests is English revolutions: anything from Boadicea's uprising to the suffragette movement. I classify these as revolutions on the grounds that only success confers the title of revolution on what is otherwise dismissed by historians as a revolt or an uprising.

Not having been around at the time, to picture the actual events, I have only been able to photograph the statues erected to the English revolutionaries. (And it is surprising how many statues there are to these English revolutionaries; there are several within yards of the Houses of Parliament.)

As I have said before, statues are good subjects for photographs — they don't move, they don't complain, and they don't ask for payment.

Figure 3.3 reproduces an illustrated article of mine, from a free magazine called *TNT*. The article includes pictures of revolutionary statues; all the pictures have sold more than once — with broadly similar articles in other magazines.

But enough of statues and the like. The writer-photographer should also collect 'record' shots: the sort of photographs that are used as picture postcards. Everyone likes to see an overall picture of a town or scene, or a typical street scene, or a picturesque old building. And editors are just like ordinary people. (Yes, really.)

When visiting a new or otherwise interesting town, make a bee-line for the racks of postcards. Notice what they show — and go off and re-photograph them yourself. You will usually be able to include a straight-

Statues of Dissent

by Gordon Wells

Most radical-minded visitors to London are aware of, and visit, the Karl Marx memorial in Highgate Cemetery. But staid old, conservative, reactionary, London has more than just the bust of Marx for the revolutionary historian to see.

It seems almost as though London delights in raising memorials to its favourite revolutionaries. Which other country would countenance a statue of the commoner who beheaded its king ... within the bounds of the Palace of Westminster? Yet there stands Oliver Cromwell, the Lord Protector — warts and all — facing out onto Parliament Square.

Cromwell's statue, by Sir William Hamo Thorneycroft, was erected in 1899 at the instigation of the Liberal Party of the time. But because of the opposition of Irish MPs — and remember, Cromwell crushed all Irish opposition with considerable vigour — it was paid for personally by Lord Roseberry, the then Prime Minister.

Less than a quarter of a mile from Oliver Cromwell's statue stands that of Boadicea. Or should it be Boudicca? In her day, Boadicea rose in righteous revolt against the Roman rulers of Britain. It seems that when her husband, King Prasutagas of the East Anglian Iceni tribe, died, he expected her to carry on in his stead. But the Romans of 61AD had never heard of Women's Lib and certainly had no intention of supporting a queen.

Instead — and probably not so planned by Rome — Boadicea is said to have been forced to witness the rape of her daughters by the licentious soldiery and had all of her husband's kingdom confiscated by petty Roman bureaucrats. Understandably, Boadicea called upon her people to rise with her, in revolt against their Roman overlords.

Initially, Boadicea's Celtic tribesmen gave the Roman Legions a lot of very bloody noses she and her rampaging Celts massacred the Roman IXth Legion, destroyed the Roman settlement at Colchester, and captured London. But perhaps inevitably, she was eventually defeated, somewhere north of St Albans. She herself committed suicide rather than be captured by the Romans; few of her Celts survived to tell of their defeat.

Whatever her fate, she is today a British heroine and her memory is glorified in a fine, if quite unrealistic, statue at the northern abutment of Westminster Bridge. This statue was sculpted by Thomas Thorneycroft and erected in the Victorian heyday of 1902. It is interesting to note that Boadicea controls her fearsome horses without reins.

With a more revolutionary connection, and less obviously visible, is the London Stone. In 1450, Jack Cade, who was said at the time to be illegitimately related to the House of York, led the ordinary people of Kent and Sussex in revolt against King Henry VI's corrupt Lancastrian advisers.

Initially, Jack Cade's revolt was successful and his peasant 'army' took control of London. In the fashion of the day, Jack Cade touched his sword to the London Stone and, in the presence of the Lord Mayor, declared himself 'Lord of London'. In 1450 the London Stone stood in the middle of what is now Cannon Street; today it — or what's left of it — rests behind a grille in the wall of the Chinese Bank in Cannon Street, just opposite the station.

Despite their early successes though, Jack Cade's army was beaten in a bloody, night-long,

Fig. 3.3

A reproduction of the author's illustrated feature article "Statues of Dissent" as used in TNT *Magazine. Several of the pictures have been published more than once.*

In prison, she would go on hunger strike until she was too weak to remain in custody. Then the authorities would release her — only to re-arrest her as soon as she had regained her strength. She would once again refuse to eat, and in time, would again be released ... and so on.

Emmeline Pankhurst made a considerable nuisance of herself. It was in great part due to her activities that the women of Britain were given the vote in 1918. And it was Emmeline Pankhurst who told an American audience that, 'Nothing has even been got out of the British parliament without something nearly approaching a revolution!'.

For all Mrs Pankhurst's radical activities though it was Stanley Baldwin, the Liberal prime minister of the day, who unveiled the statue to this brave woman in 1930. She believed in the British Parliamentary processes.

Karl Marx may have written about revolution, but Emmeline Pankhurst — along with the other British revolutionaries remembered in London's statues — really suffered for her cause. They have earned their statues.

battle fought out across a burning London Bridge. The peasants were then tricked into accepting worthless and inappropriate pardons and returning home. Cade found himself abandoned by his supporters; he fled, hunted by the King's men across Kent and Sussex; he was finally killed by the Sheriff of Kent, in a garden near Heathfield in East Sussex. (There is a stone memorial to the event by the roadside there, in the aptly-named hamlet of Cade Street.)

Suffragettes

You do not need to leave central London though for another statuesque reminder of Britain's revolutionary past. Close to the Palace of Westminster, in Victoria Tower Gardens, stands a statue to Emmeline Pankhurst. to look at, she appears to be just another rther frail middle-class lady. But this frail middle-class lady led the women of Britain in a long — and hard-fought — battle to earn themselves the right to vote. Emmeline Pankhurst was the founder and the frontline leader of the Women's Social and Political Union — the Suffragettes.

In the beginning, when she founded the WSPU in her Manchester parlour, Mrs Pankhurst believed in petitioning and lobbying Parliament. She also staged mass public meetings and women's marches in London. But the Liberal Governments of the day took little note of these troublesome women. So the suffragette agitation was stepped up.

Before the 1914-18 war temporarily swept aside all thoughts of an extended suffrage, Mrs Pankhurst and her dedicated followers became more and more militant. She herself was repeatedly arrested and imprisoned.

The statue of Oliver Cromwell, the Lord Protector, which stands inside the grounds of the Palace of Westminster, looking out onto Parliament Square

Emmeline Pankhurst points delicately towards the House of Parliament — which for so long denied her and her fellow women, the vote. She died two years before the statue was erected

forward record shot with almost every illustrated article.

Look now at the pictures which sold with the travel article reproduced at Figure 3.4; these, with the possible exception of the street scene, are classic picture-postcard shots; they were essential accompaniments for this article though. (And even here, in 'picture-post-card land', notice that I have still taken, and sold, upright pictures in preference to landscape.)

Action poses

Moving away now from statues and other inanimate objects, there was the article in *The Lady* about cockle-fishing. Here the pictures were of people. People at work. Such pictures too are meat and drink to features editors. Editors like features about craftspeople — and they like the pictures to show the subject at work.

Some years ago, while working abroad, I photo-graphed an elderly woman using an unusual technique (known as the 'hammer and anvil' method of pottery) to make an earthenware flask; in my overseas markets I sold this picture several times. It is reproduced at Figure 3.5 — along with another picture, of the product she was making.

It is always a good idea to include a picture of the end result along with any picture of someone at work. It finishes off the story. Sometimes, you can include the finished product — such as a drawing or painting — within the main picture.

Pictures of people at work can sometimes be taken *candidly* — ie 'snatched', without artificially posing the subject — but this is not easy; more often, some direction of the subject, by the photographer, into a 'natural'

Why Cahors has a Lot to offer

by
Gordon Wells

Ideally, you should approach Cahors from the air, where you appreciate immediately how strong and important the town once was, guarding a hairpin bend in the river.

The River Lot is wide here and forms a moat almost surrounding the town which in mediaeval times meant Cahors was a virtually impregnable fortress town.

In the early years of the Hundred Year War, the inhabitants of Cahors held out against the British while all the surrounding areas fell to the invaders. Then, in 1360, under the Treaty of Bretigny, the town was ceded to the British but the townspeople refused to submit until ordered by their king to hand over the keys of the city. Thereafter, Cahors was ruled by the British until 1450.

Today, most visitors arrive by road – and in peace. Cahors has much to offer the visitor, and is an excellent centre for exploring the surrounding countryside. There are several good three-star hotels – we stayed at the comfortable Hotel Wilson in the town centre – and some good restaurants too.

Cahors, the erstwhile capital town of the Quercy region, is truffle and *foie gras* territory. The many signs at the town approaches never let you forget this.

One of the most interesting architectural features of Cahors is the imposing fourteenth century Valentre Bridge with its three tall defensive towers. Incomplete, it still served its purpose in the Hundred Years War and there is, inevitably, a legend about it.

The bridge took 50 years to build and was completed about 1360. The architect, frustrated at the builders' slowness ('twas ever thus), made a pact with the Devil. If the Devil would deliver all the building materials quickly, he should have the architect's soul. But the architect craftily specified that the water be transported in a sieve.

Eventually the Devil gave up but in revenge he repeatedly dislodged the topmost stone in the centre tower. It was only when the bridge was restored, around 1880, that the stone was sufficiently well fixed to resist the Devil's efforts.

The centre tower now boasts a small carved demon still striving to dislodge the recalcitrant stone. Look for it with binoculars.

On the other side of the town, facing the river, stands the fifteenth century house once occupied by the King of Navarre, Henry IV. A fine building typical of the region, with a rose window, exposed woodwork and an outside balcony, it is now called the Maison de Roaldes (the Roaldes are a well-known local family).

Stroll through the narrow streets of the older part of Cahors to the Cathedral of St Etienne which was built between the twelfth and fourteenth centuries. There is a typical French street market every Wednesday in the square outside the cathedral, the Place Chapou. On most other days, too, there are a few market stalls there.

We bought a few bottles of the characteristic and slightly peppery Quercy vin de pays in this open-air market. Dated 1986

St Circ Lapopie, one of the prettiest villages in France

but, inevitably, without benefit of *appellation controllée*, we bought it from the producer for just £1.60 per bottle. I can vouch for its ability to travel not for its keeping qualities – because we drank it after our return.

We found some better quality local wine in the covered market near by. Vintners Le Chai en Quercy have a regular stall there, with a remarkably catholic selection of wines. Among other wines, we bought from here a fine black-labelled 1985 Chateau Vincens, a Cahors wine. These better wines are not cheap, though, reckon on paying at least £3 a bottle.

My recommendation is that the visitor should not just stay in Cahors but explore the valley of the Lot. Less well-known than the Dordogne nearby, the Lot is not so commercialised – and the better for it.

Only 12 miles from Cahors (along the D662 road) is the hillside-hugging village of St-Circ Lapopie, which is officially listed as one of the most beautiful villages of France. It has narrow winding streets, old buildings

and a spectacular view of the Lot.

An even greater potential attraction to the visitor is the Grotto of Pech Merle. The Pech Merle caves are reached from the D662 road, but you have to turn off to the north through the small village of Cabrerets.

At Pech Merle you will find a labyrinth of natural caves which make up a fantasy world of pastel-coloured stalacmites and stalactites, sometimes dripping with subterranean water. If this were not enough there is a veritable treasure house of prehistoric wall drawings.

We saw drawings of mammoths, bison and elephants, alive in their simplicity, and often striking in their perspective. There were full-size paintings of lifelike horses and, perhaps most fascinating of all, we saw "negative" silhouettes of twenty-thousand-year-old hands, outlined with paint sprayed from the mouths of prehistoric man. Personal "signatures" from pre-history. And we saw the small footprints of perhaps these

High Street, Rocamadour

Fig. 3.4   *A reproduction of an illustrated article by the author which was published in the magazine* Channel Express. *Notice the type of pictures selected by the editor – from the complete roll of film – to accompany the article.*

mall prehistoric men in the now-solidified mud. Interestingly, some of the wall drawings are superimposed on even earlier drawings.

Too much exposure to artificial light would damage these prehistoric relics so the public is taken on tours of the caves in groups of no more than 25 at a time and only restricted number are allowed into the caves each day.

As you pass around the caves the route head is briefly illuminated by the young and enthusiastic guides, as soon as you pass through a section the lights go out. Photography is prohibited.

A visit to Cahors would be worthwhile just for the opportunity of seeing the caves and paintings at Pech Merle, which are unforgettable.

Yet Cahors is also an ideal centre for ranging further afield. Within comfortable motoring distance of Cahors are the underground caves and lake at Padirac (much more commercialised than Pech Merle, but well worth visiting), the ancient religious centre of Rocamadour, clinging to the hillside, and all the glorious scenery along the undiscovered valley of the Lot.

Pont de Valentre at Cahors

DON'T BRING BACK TOO MUCH

will come as no surprise that there are certain items that should not be brought into this country from abroad. Restrictions and guidelines have been imposed to protect us, our wildlife and environment from a number of animal and plant diseases that have not yet taken hold here.

For instance, fresh cream cakes are a no-go area!

The one disease which most of us are aware of is rabies. It is widespread throughout the world and can kill humans and animals if not treated in time. Britain has been free of the disease for over 60 years and if we continue to observe simple rules we may be able to keep things that way.

Nearly all animals coming to Britain – and that includes any animals you take with you abroad and subsequently want to bring back – must spend six months in quarantine. This rule applies equally to animals on board a ship or aircraft which has been diverted to a destination outside Britain unexpectedly because of bad weather.

If you are found smuggling any animal or bird into Britain you can be heavily fined – up to £2,000 – or sent to prison. So do not be tempted to bring back stray or other live animals from abroad. If you do intend to import any animal prepare for its arrival in advance. You will have to obtain a licence from the Ministry of Agriculture Fisheries and Food and expect to pay considerable board and lodging charges while the animal is in quarantine.

Remember if you are bitten or scratched by an animal while you are abroad it is vital for your own protection to follow this advice.

● Take the name, address and telephone number of the owner of the animal. If this is not possible, ask the local police to trace the animal urgently

● Find out if the animal is healthy and has been vaccinated against rabies

● Ask to be informed if the animal becomes unwell over the next two weeks

● Wash the wound immediately with soap and water and see a doctor at once. You may need preventive treatment for rabies

● See your own doctor immediately you return home, even if the wound does not look bad. Do not take any chances.

When you are shopping abroad, it may be tempting to bring home many of the foods and delicacies you see in the shops and markets, particularly if you have sampled a food you enjoyed in a restaurant.

There are regulations, however, on bringing in items such as meat. You are only allowed to bring back 1.2 lb of fully-cooked meat packaged in cans, sealed glass jars or flexible airtight pouches. However tempting, do not bring back pate, salami or uncooked meat such as sausages. They are not permitted.

You can bring back up to 4.4 lb of fruit or vegetables but please remember, potatoes are not permitted. You are allowed a small bouquet of cut flowers (but not chrysanthemums since they are subject to a disease not yet established in this country), and up to 11 lb of tubers, bulbs and corms free of soil. You can also bring back up to five retail packets of seeds.

Parsley and spinach can sometimes carry colorado beetle. The adult beetle is less than half an inch long with black and yellow lines running front to back. If introduced into Britain, this pest could seriously damage our potato crops. So watch out for it on any vegetables you might buy.

There are still plenty of unrestricted items which you can bring home. There is all the mouth-watering cheeses, butter, bread, croissants, pastries and delicious cakes. Milk and cream however is not allowed so if you do buy cakes just make sure that they do not have fresh cream in them.

The best advice to follow, if you are unsure of something which you have bought, is to declare it to customs.

A "craftsperson at work" photograph – always saleable – accompanied by a picture (inset) of the finished product.

pose is needed. This was not possible with my potter-lady; luckily though, she ignored me.

The important thing when posing a craftsperson at work is to make them appear to be working. And to make sure they don't ogle the camera. They should be looking at what they are doing — not at you. And you will concentrate your camera on the action — ie, the hands — while at the same time, keeping a watch on the face for a particularly absorbed expression.

Picturing artefacts etc.

Another popular subject for feature articles by the average writer-photographer is 'collectibles'. Many an article has been sold about unusual door-knockers, about pieces of jade, about old coins, about fine porcelain figurines, or about carvings in wood, bone, ivory

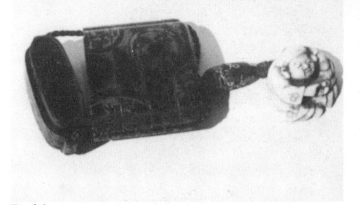

Fig. 3.6

A close-up photograph of a group of linked artefacts. (A netsuke, *an* inro, *and an* ojme.*) Notice how the artefacts fill the frame – with little concern for formal composition.*

or . . . And such articles MUST be accompanied by relevant photographs.

If you are about to write and illustrate a 'collectibles' article, you can more or less forget about composition. All that the editor requires is a set of good, big, clear pictures of whatever the article is about. And to achieve good, big, clear pictures there are a few words of advice:

- get in close — almost certainly using a *macro* lens or close-up adaptor rings (but if not using an SLR camera, watch out for viewfinder parallax).

    However you achieve it, fill the picture frame with the subject. And don't confuse the viewer by trying to put too much into one picture.

    Figure 3.6 shows a complete set of linked arte- facts: the open *inro* (the box which did duty for a pocket in Japan), the bead-like *ojme* which holds the *inro* shut, and the *netsuke* which retains the

73

inro and *ojme* as they hang from a belt. (Had I attempted any formal composition — such as arranging the set to spread diagonally across the frame — I would have been in danger of producing a less-sharply focussed picture. Clarity is of paramount importance.) The illustration is an enlargement of virtually the whole of the negative — I filled the frame.

The picture illustrated an article about collecting *netsuke*. There were, of course, several other pictures of *netsuke* alone.

- provide yourself with a plain background against which to photograph the artefacts.

I sometimes use a large sheet of green card, pale on one side, for dark subjects — and darker on the other, for lighter-coloured subjects. I find a stark white card can often be too harsh. (But it was right, for Figure 3.6.)

- ensure that the lighting is such that it will emphasise the features of the artefact.

A deeply carved subject will usually benefit from *properly balanced* side lighting — to produce light and shade. Lighting from one side only could well be over-contrasty and lead to lack of detail in the shaded portions of the picture. At the same time, a flat subject might be better photographed with flat lighting.

I have photographed many such small artefacts — including the *inro, ojme, netsuke* set for example — in the open air using slightly overcast sunlight, which retains its directional quality without generating over-harsh shadows.

Another possibility — if you are in the business of photographing a lot of *macro* type subjects — is to invest in a *ringflash*. This is a conventional electronic flash, but the tube encircles the lens giving truly flat light. And the output can be regulated. But ringflashes are expensive; don't buy one if you don't need one. I have long managed without.

Children and animals

As any Thespian knows, children and/or animals can steal a scene as soon as they walk on. For exactly the same reason, every writer-photographer worth their salt will be permanently on the lookout for pictorial opportunities featuring kids and/or animals. We have already mentioned how my son feeding the dragon *makes* the picture.

I was out taking 'striking portraits' for a newspaper series I was running. I had persuaded a handsome tribesman to pose for me. Just as I clicked the shutter though, up popped an urchin with his (coated) tongue sticking out. Far from spoiling the shot, as I at first thought, it made it. See Figure 3.7: This has sold several times, all over the world.

Personally, I'm not much good at photographing animals. Maybe I lack the patience. But the classic advice undoubtedly applies: do as I say, not as I do. Be on the look out for any picture opportunity including an animal. Such pictures will almost always sell.

Portraits

The writer-photographer will not have a lot of use for straightforward portrait photography. Normally, this is best left to the specialist professional. When a writer-

Fig. 3.7

An accident. My intention was a straight portrait of the tribesman at the rear. The young urchin popped up at just the wrong – but actually just the right – moment. The urchin "makes" the picture, which has sold several times.

photographer needs to photograph someone to accompany a related feature article, it is usually wisest to portray them at work. But there will sometimes be the need for a straight 'mug shot'.

I had such a need when I interviewed a fellow writer for a writing magazine. I was asked for a portrait; I thought that if I provided a particularly good one, it might make the cover of the magazine. I was right, I tried hard, it did. (I have only ever sold two or three magazine cover photographs — and this was one. So I was quite pleased.)

I took the easy way out; I photographed my friend outdoors, in fairly bright sunshine, and selected a good dark background in order to emphasise the side-lit face and hair. It was an occasion which seemed to need fill-

Fig. 3.8

A natural light portrait of my writer friend Donna Baker which was used on the cover of Writers' Monthly. *It was associated with a report of an interview with her – by me.*

in flash. So I took some shots with flash and some without. The chosen cover picture, shown at Figure 3.8 was one of the non-flashed ones; one with fill-in flash was used with the interview article itself on an inside page. (The actual cover, of *Writers' Monthly*, could not be reproduced, for technical reasons.)

Again, this demonstrates the advantages of taking several shots for each required picture. It is always best to have — and to offer the editor — a choice.

Picturing the unusual

If there is one single type of subject which almost guarantees a saleable picture, it is the unusual. Magazine readers are always interested in anything unusual, anything different, anything that makes them stop and marvel — or chuckle. And the unusualness does not need to be really staggering: a couple of juxtaposed signs creating a puerile *double entendre* is ample.

I have twice (so far) sold a picture of a strangely decorated house in my home village. And this has not even entailed writing an article; it sold once as a 'stand alone' picture and once as an accompaniment to a 'Letter to the Editor'. It is reproduced at Figure 3.9.

As a writer-photographer, every single time you see anything unusual, you should take a picture. It might not be there next time you pass. (I have often kicked myself mentally, for failing to photograph a simple sign that said, 'This bridge is unsafe by order of the Director of Public Works.' Nothing much — but it would surely have covered my film costs for several weeks.)

Being driven along a road in China, on holiday a year or so ago, I was fascinated by the haystacks hanging from the roadside trees. Eventually, I persuaded the coach driver to stop and let me grab a quick picture. It has already sold twice and I can see several other potential sales. It's unusual.

The 'haystack tree' has just recently been sold again, as an accompaniment to a 'Letter to the Editor' of *Country Life*. (They don't pay for letters; they do pay for the pictures.) It is reproduced, with my letter, at Figure 3.10.

I was impressed recently too, by an illustrated article by a competing writer-photographer — in *The Lady*. It was all about unusual street name-plates. Some of the names were very amusing. It was the sort of feature that I could have produced standing on my head — if I had had the idea. I didn't; my competitor did. It was an excellent use of *a set* of unusual photographs.

Fig. 3.9

The unusual "Cat House" in my home village. I have sold this photograph to the local county magazine and accompanying a "Letter to the Editor".

- August 19--

The Editor
Country Life
King's Reach Tower
Stamford Street
London SE1 9LS

Dear Madam

Like many of your readers, I well remember when
beautifully-made haystcks were a decorative
feature of the English countryside. Today though,
all one ever sees are rolls of mechanically packed
hay - sometimes even wrapped up in black plastic
sheets. Efficient but hardly attractive.

Today's efficient farmers may nevertheless be
interested in the enclosed picture of a "haystack
tree" which I saw recently, in China - before the
Tian An Men Square revolt. The picture shows how
ever scrap of land is used for cultivation and how
the hay is then hung from the trees to keep it safe
from flooding. Both efficient and picturesque.

Maybe the next stage here will be to suspend our
haystacks from trees? That might even save the
cost of the black plastic bin-liners.

Yours faithfully

Gordon Wells

Gordon Wells

(I would much appreciate the return of the
photograph. I enclose a stamped addressed
envelope for this purpose.)   Fig. 3.10

*A "haystack tree" seen in China. This has been sold as an illustration to an
article about holidaying in China. It has also recently sold to* Country Life
*as an accompaniment to a "Letter to the Editor". My accompanying letter
is also reproduced.*

The saleability of the unusual picture acknowledged, the taking of it depends on two things:

- the writer-photographer needs to cultivate an eagle eye for 'the unusual' (refurbish your schoolboy/girl sense of humour) — and don't overlook the possibilities of even moving a sign to juxtapose it more interestingly;
- the writer-photographer needs to carry a camera — possibly just a compact — at all times, ready for the unrepeatable shot. (Beware though, a car's glovebox can be ruinously hot, even in a British summer.)

The unusual shot is also a possible contender for entering in photographic competitions.

Competitions

Writer-photographers should not overlook photographic competitions. Just because you are a writer, taking the odd photograph to complement your writing, does not mean that you should ignore the possibilities of 'Happy Snap' competitions. Your experience of taking saleable pictures will probably stand you in good stead in such competitions.

What sort of pictures make good competition entries?

First and foremost, the judges are looking for entries that abide by the competition rules. If you actually note the organisers' rules and regulations — and abide by them — you will have a head start over most of the 'ordinary' competitors. (If they ask for entries to be accompanied by three product labels, give them their three labels; if they want seaside pictures, don't send them a picture of a farmyard scene, no matter how good; if they want colour prints, don't send them black and white prints — or colour transparencies.)

Secondly, go for a happy picture whenever possible — and children at play are ideal. Lots of sunshine helps too, in most competitions. Almost always, your entry should be of people — landscapes are seldom called for.

Thirdly, make sure that the subject of the picture is doing something. Competition judges seldom want straight portraits — even if you do think that little Willy is a lovely looking child.

Further, and more detailed, advice on entering photographic competitions is given in Chapter 6.

What not to take

Finally, in this review of the sort of pictures that are most likely to help you, as a writer-photographer, sell your articles — what not to take.

Remember what you are. You are not — and the purpose of this book is certainly not to advise you how to become — a press photographer. First and foremost, you are a writer; your photographic objective is to enhance the sales of your written work. With that reminder, the list of what not to take is easy to compile.

Unless a major pop star or a member of the Royal Family drops dead, or falls off a horse, immediately in front of you — and preferably only you — don't attempt to photograph celebrities. (Other than, of course, a 'mug shot' in the context of an interview.) The press photographers have far better facilities for photographing people in the news — and they can get their films processed faster than you can unload the camera.

(If however, you are lucky enough to be the only camera-equipped observer at a Royal tumble or celebrity catastrophe, snap away like mad. Take lots of pictures — from all angles, not forgetting an overall shot of the scene and plenty of close-ups. Make sure that you get the names of all those involved too — pictures have to have captions.

(Finish the roll of film. BUT DON'T DASH OFF AND PROCESS IT. Find a phone. Call one of the bigger London newspapers — or one of the agencies — and tell them what you've got. If they are interested, they will advise you how to despatch the unprocessed film direct to them — probably by passenger train if outside London.

(The newspaper will process the film and make any necessary prints. While you are on the phone to them, prior to despatch, don't forget also, to talk about payment, subject to the pictures being usable. If they are good — and interesting — they could make a really big front-page splash. And they should pay you handsomely for their exclusive use, your *scoop*. But such miracles only happen once in a lifetime — if then. I'm still waiting for my scoop.)

So, basically — forget news pictures. Don't waste your time taking popular sports action pictures either. (But again, the caveat: if there is a really spectacular accident just in front of you — and preferably far from other photographers — photograph it and act as above.) The gentlemen from the Press will always — and rightly — have the best spots from which to photograph. They will also have powerful telephoto lenses.

Don't waste time taking photographs of glamorous — inevitably unclad — girls, either. (I suppose there is no reason why you shouldn't take them, for your own amusement. But a writer-photographer is, by definition, not in the 'Page 3' photography business.) 'In the business' or not though, the ordinary writer-photographer is unlikely to be able to produce the exaggerated and glitzy photographs used on 'Page 3'.

Summary

Because this chapter is of particular importance to the writer-photographer, it is worth summarising some of its more significant content. Pictures for a writer-photographer to take, to stand the best chance of achieving 'words and pictures package' sales should:

- be both upright and landscape as appropriate — NOT all landscape;
- preferably be collected in 'sets';
- often duplicate the subjects of local picture post-card shots; (if you are going to write about Mudch-ester Abbey, a straightforward picture-postcard type view of the Abbey will enhance the chances of making a sale.)
- ideally be related to subjects already researched for writing about;
- show a single, well-defined subject, large and clear, filling the frame;
- wherever appropriate, be well-composed, but not at the expense of 'large and clear' — in other words, don't try to be too 'arty-crafty';
- be technically excellent — pin-sharp focus, with plenty of detail, and accurately exposed;
- wherever possible/relevant, include people — who

should preferably be doing something — and children are even better;
- be of the unusual, or the humorous, or just the interesting;
- NOT be of news, sports or glamour subjects.

4

THE PROCESSING PROCESS

You have taken the last picture on your roll of film.
So far, it's all been relatively painless. Now what do
you do?

The first thing, of course, is to take the film out of
the camera. You can't just open the back and remove
the tin box containing the film. First — the film is no
longer in the *cassette*; it is rolled around a spool within
the camera. If you open the back of the camera now,
all the film will be ruined by exposure to the light.
So . . . first of all, you must rewind the film — wind it
back into its little tin box, its cassette.

With the newer, more automatic cameras, the
camera itself senses when the film is completed — and
rewinds the film for you, without any action on your
part. But this is only on the more sophisticated of
cameras.

With most cameras, the writer-photographer will
need to press a button (often on the base of the camera)

to free the winding mechanism, and then actually wind the film back. The winder usually unfolds at the top of the camera above the cassette position.

Once the film is back in the cassette — either by your winding it back yourself or automatically — you can open the back of the camera and remove the cassette. Now comes the crunch. What do you do with that cassette?

With 'happy snaps' in colour, there is no problem. You either take the film to a High Street film processing shop, or post it off to one of the several firms who specialise in mail-order processing. You pay a few pounds (usually less than a fiver) and back come your pictures, all beautifully enlarged to 6″ × 4″. From the High Street processor, you can get the pictures back in just an hour — but it will cost you more. By mail order, the prints are returned within about a week. Often you get a 'free' replacement film thrown in. It's all very easy.

But colour photography is a mass-market hobby. These days, only a minority of photographers work in black and white. Few of the High Street or mail order operators go out of their way to make life easy for this comparative handful of specialist photographers.

There are three alternatives for the writer-photographer needing to get black and white film processed:

- go to a specialist black and white film processor;
- process the film yourself;
- use an unusual black and white film that is designed to be handled by the mass colour film processors.

Specialist film processors

Buy an up-to-date issue of *Amateur Photographer* (or any of the other photographic magazines — but the *AP* usually has the most advertisements); in the classified advertisement pages at the back of the magazine there will be a number of black and white film processing services. But they look expensive.

To someone used to having colour film processed, they undoubtedly are expensive. Whereas a 36-exposure colour film can be processed to 'Super-Enprints' for a few pence under five pounds (and often with a 'free' film too), a similar black and white 'package' service will cost around eight pounds. And that's a lot more.

One 'solution' which I have sometimes used myself is to opt for even bigger enprints. Get the black and white enprints made at the usually offered (but about fifty percent more expensive — £12) 5″ × 7″ size — and submit these with your articles. (*See* the next chapter for advice on how to submit pictures to editors.)

This 5″ × 7″ enprint approach, to be economically sensible, requires you to have great confidence in your ability to produce well-framed, full-negative, pictures — all the time. If you can use at least fifty percent of your exposures as article-illustrations, the larger package price is worth paying. (Eighteen saleable pictures within a £12 package means an acceptable 67 pence per picture; if you can only use six of your pictures though, the unit cost becomes £2 — which is quite uneconomic.)

I have used this approach when I have photographed a whole set of small artefacts — jade and ivory carvings and small Asian bronzes, for example — to illustrate a series of articles on linked subjects. I *knew* that all the photographs were sharp, well-lit and *saleable*. It was an economical way of getting the prints I needed. However, I would not have used this approach for eg travel pictures where I tend to take a wide variety of pictures — and only use a small proportion of them. You must decide for yourself when and whether to go down the enprint route.

But the 'enprint package' is probably not the best way of having all your black and white film processed. Look more closely at the services offered by the advertisers. They will almost always also offer something like 'Dev and cp' or 'Dev and 10″ × 8″ contact' — and the price for this service will usually be less than £3, including postage. This is the service you should go for.

A 'develop and contact print' service includes — of course — the development of the film; the contact print is a single 10″ × 8″ sheet showing all of the 36 pictures on the roll of film — each approximately 1½″ × 1″. The negatives are not individually printed — the whole film is printed at one time with a single overall exposure. Figure 4.1 shows a typical 10″ × 8″ contact print sheet.

(With an enprint package, each picture is given an appropriate overall exposure; by comparison, with a top-quality one-off enlargement, areas of the negative are differentially exposed to improve the overall result)

Given a contact sheet, what do you do with it? You need a powerful magnifying glass. With this, you can inspect the tiny prints and select the best for separate enlargement. You can also decide whether the final print should be made from only a part of the exposed negative. The picture may thereby be improved.

(I pride myself on composing virtually all my pictures in the viewfinder, but on some occasions the negatives

Fig. 4.1

A typical 10" x 8" contact print – showing the whole of a 36-exposure roll of 35 mm film.

90

can still be improved by selective enlarging. Try to adopt this approach yourself. It is always best to use as much of the tiny negative as possible — it improves the sharpness and general quality, and minimises the graininess of the print.)

You then return the negatives, or send them elsewhere, (still in probably six-picture-long strips) for enlarging. If you want enlargements of the full negatives you will not need to return the contact sheet; if you want only a part enlargement, you can mark the revised frame boundaries on the contact sheet and return it as a guide to the processor. (Mark the contact sheet with a Chinagraph or similar greasy pencil.)

You will want the enlargements to be at least 7″ × 5″ and possibly 10″ × 8″ — we will discuss 'the best' size for enlargements later in this chapter. Each 7″ × 5″ enlargement will cost (early 1990) around 60 pence and a 10″ × 8″ about twice that.

Six usable pictures from the 'dev and cp' package, enlarged to 7″ × 5″ will therefore have cost around £1.20 each. (£3 for the 'dev and cp' equals 50 pence for each of the eventual six prints, plus say 60 pence for the enlargement and 10 pence towards postage: total £1.20.) This compares very favourably with the £2 per print cost that we calculated for going down the 'super-enprint package' route as outlined above.

A further 'plus' for the 'develop and contact print' approach to film processing is that you have a permanent record of all the pictures on a roll of film. No matter how many enlargements you sell, the whole film remains viewable on the contact sheet. We will discuss below a suitable filing system incorporating the contact sheet.

After trying several black and white develop and print services, I have settled down to using just one

91

good one. Not the cheapest, but very good quality and speedy. I use, and recommend:

Classic Photography Service
Walton Cottage
Ebrey Wood
Astley, Shrewsbury SY4 4DE.

Self-processing

Only the dedicated enthusiast need read this next section. No one actually *needs* to process their own black and white films. But there are some benefits from self-processing.

It is possible to develop an important roll of film yourself, the same day that you expose it; the developing process will take less than an hour of your time. And once the film is developed — and dry — you can then immediately send selected negatives off to a film processing service for enlargement. Processing your own films will be cheaper than the 'developing' element of the 'dev and cp' prices. And, perhaps more important, you will save several days.

A further potential benefit from self-processing is that you can develop short lengths of film. But this depends on your loading short lengths of film into the camera. Or you can 'push' the film speed by extra developing — to compensate for insufficient light perhaps. But both 'rolling your own' films and 'speed-pushing' are too sophisticated for the ordinary writer-photographer. Don't bother with them.

The really big financial savings come from doing your own enlargements. But to do this you need a fully equipped darkroom — and you will find yourself spending many hours peering at slowly appearing images in a dish of developer. This is fine for an enthusiastic photographer — but you are a writer-photographer — your main interest should be in the writing.

Don't bother with making your own enlargements; get them done for you.

So now, a quick run through of the film developing process — for the really keen reader. First, the equipment. You will need:

- a light-proof 35 mm developing tank;
- a bottle each of developer, stop-bath and fixer — at the correct dilution for use;
- a thermometer and a timer (your watch may suffice);
- a graduated beaker (or two)— ie with liquid quantities marked on it;
- a couple of film clips — one for each end of the film; and perhaps, as discussed below,
- a 'portable darkroom', a light-tight changing bag.

You will also need access to running water — the kitchen sink or a convenient bathroom.

The process of developing your own film consists, briefly, of the following steps:

- Load the film. Within a darkened, totally light-proof room (inside a walk-in cupboard perhaps), or by using a light-tight changing bag, open the film cassette and load the exposed film into the spiral of the developing tank.

  (Practise loading the spiral with a length of scrap film in broad daylight. There is a knack to feeding the film in around the spiral guides. With a plastic reel, you rotate the top and bottom spirals alternately, feeding the film in from the outside; with a fixed stainless steel spiral you have to clip the end of the film to the centre of the reel and then load the spiral by bowing the film so that it springs into place in the reel.)

Place the loaded spiral in the developing tank and screw on the lid. You can now come out from the darkroom or dispense with the changing bag. All other operations are done in ordinary lighting.

(A changing bag consists of a large, double-zipped bag made of thick light-proof cloth, with two elasticated sleeves. You put the cassette of film and the developing tank and spiral into the bag and zip it shut. Then you put your hands into the bag, through the sleeves, and working by feel, open the cassette (the end prises off), load the film into the spiral, insert it into the tank, and close the tank lid. You can then remove your arms, unzip the bag and remove the light-tight tank. You are more constrained, working within a changing bag, and you should practise using them, but they are ideal when away from home.)

- Prepare the chemicals. Dilute the developer as instructed on the relevant label. (It is sensible, initially at least, to use a general-purpose liquid developer until you become accustomed to messing about with the chemicals.)

Check the temperature of the liquid and if it is not within the temperature range specified on the developer label (around 20 deg C, 68 deg F), put the beaker full of developer in a bowl of warm water — or, less likely, of ice cubes.

Prepare — usually dilute — the other chemicals, the stop-bath and the fixer, in accordance with the instructions on their labels. Stop-bath and fixer should be around the same temperature as the developer but their temperatures are not quite so critical.

- Pour the developer into the closed tank and start the timer. (It is also worth banging the developing tank two or three times, fairly smartly, on the table — to dislodge any air bubbles locked between layers of film.) The tank should now be agitated, by inverting it repeatedly, in a regular fashion, for about 5 seconds, at 30-second intervals.

- Pour off the developer liquid. (Some developers are saved for re-use, other discarded.) Start pouring off the liquid about ten seconds before the specified completion time, to ensure that the tank is emptied on time.

- Straight away, pour in the stop-bath and agitate continuously for about 30 seconds. This ensures that the inevitable residual coating of developer does not continue to act on the film. Pour off the stop-bath.

- Pour in the fixer and leave for the time specified in the fixer instructions, agitating occasionally. At the end of the time, pour off the fixer — it can probably be re-used, but be careful, don't re-use it too often. (Don't be mean with it.)

- Wash the film, preferably still in the tank, but with the top removed. Ideally, direct running water down through the centre of the spiral; alternatively, the film and spiral can be removed from the tank and washed in the same way but in a large dish. At a pinch, but to be avoided (running water is vastly preferable), the film can be washed in the tank, by several changes of poured-in water.

- At the end of the wash, add a few drops of wetting

agent to the still-full tank (or dish) and agitate it
gently.

- Remove the loaded reel from tank or dish, fix a
  film-clip to the free end of the wet — but now
  safely developed — film and carefully pull it out.
  When free of the reel, fix a clip on the other end
  too.
- Holding one end by the clip, gently swab or squee-
  gee the film to get rid of surplus water. Hang it up
  to dry — in a dust-free room.
- When bone-dry, cut the film into 6-exposure strips,
  inspect them — and perhaps contact print the
  whole set — then store the negatives in individual
  wallets.

It really is quite a simple, painless process. (By far the
worst part is loading the film into the spiral reel. But
once you get the knack, that's easy too.)

As far as the equipment and chemicals are con-
cerned, any specialist photography shop will be able to
supply everything necessary. £10 should cover the lot.
The equipment, once bought, will just about last for
ever.

As a follow on to film developing, if you are really
keen — or anxious to save money — it is not difficult
to make your own contact print sheets too. The best
way to do this is to buy a contact print 'frame'. This is
usually a plastic sheet with slots into which the 6-
exposure strips of negatives can be fitted and which
provides space thereunder for a 10″ × 8″ sheet of photographic paper. You 'load' the negatives into the frame
in the daylight. Thereafter you need a darkroom.

For contact printing only, wait until it's dark and
black out a room — ideally the kitchen or bathroom.
In the dark, by the light of an inexpensive red dark-

room light, put a 10″ × 8″ sheet of photographic paper ('coated' — ie with photographic emulsion — side up) in the contact print frame. Switch on the ordinary lighting for a while, to expose the paper. (The first time, you will need to experiment with small strips of paper to get the right exposure time. Once timed though, this should remain constant.) Switch the light off again.

Develop the paper in a large purpose-made dish of print developer (which differs from film developer); then, after the specified time, when the picture has appeared, transfer it briefly to a dish of stop-bath and thereafter to a dish of fixer. After the fixer, put the print into a dish of clean water. If you're not in the bathroom or kitchen, take the water dish and the print to the running water and then wash it for several minutes.

All that is left to do now is to hang the print up to dry.

Contact printing is not difficult — but it does entail some more investment in photographic equipment. Think hard before you get involved in this. Above all, remember that you are a writer, not a photographer. If you do then decide to do your own contact printing you may well find it helpful to contact your local camera club for assistance. One practical demonstration — or better, a hand-held personal experience — will be worth a couple of chapters of book reading.

Alternatively, most of the black and white film processing services will contact print your negatives for you. The charge for this is usually around £1.50. Think about it.

An unusual film

There is a relatively new alternative to either of the above development options. This is to use Ilford's XP-1 film. This is an unusual film inasmuch as it is a black and white film *specially designed to be developed and printed by the mass-user colour process*. It is also fast (400 ASA), virtually grain-free, and has a lot of latitude to under-exposure.

The film costs about the same as any other film — but you can take it to a colour print shop, and get your black and white (almost – they have a slight sepia tinge) enprints back within hours, at colour processing prices.

The snag? Yes, there is now. Not all colour film processing laboratories will handle XP-1 film. In its early days, processing XP-1 film as part of a batch of colour films was thought to reduce the quality of the colour processing. But today, there are some firms who will process XP-1. And the situation can only get better. Ilford are 'selling' the idea of colour processing of XP-1 as hard as they can.

Boots are reported as willing to accept XP-1 for processing as colour, as are some High Street one-hour processors. My favourite (ie, the cheapest and the best) colour print processor, Truprint, will not accept XP-1 film though. I have successfully used the mail-order firm of Will R Rose, 23 Bridge Street Row, Chester CH1 1YZ. (Mark the order form or covering note carefully, 'XP-1 Film to be printed on Colour Paper', and send payment with the order.) 1989 prices were £2.95 for develop and 6″ × 4″ enprints from 24-exposure film, and £4.00 from 36-exposure film, including postage. Unfortunately though, XP-1 enprints from Will R Rose have a somewhat pronounced sepia tinge.

Of course, the specialist black and white film processors will also handle XP-1. But most charge extra for XP-1; which rather defeats the object, other than for the film's latitude, speed and fine-grain qualities.

Enlargements

However your black and white film has been processed, you will usually need enlargements to accompany your articles. The 'standard' size for enlargements for submitting to editors is 10″ × 8″. That is fine — but large prints are expensive.

The cost of a 10″ × 8″ enlargement is almost always well over £1. If you are submitting illustrated articles *on spec* you will understandably begrudge (as I do too) such an expensive gamble. Not only do 10″ × 8″ enlargements themselves cost a lot; the cost of two-way postage and secure packing increases accordingly.

I have noticed, however, that many publicity or press release photographs are supplied to editors in the form of 7″ × 5″ prints. If that is big enough for those uses, it will usually be large enough for your articles too. Certainly I have never had an editorial complaint — in respect of an illustration for an unsolicited feature article — about my submitting 7″ × 5″ prints.

There are two qualifications to that comment:

- the subject of the picture must be large within the frame — but that's a standard requirement; and
- the picture is unlikely to be printed larger than the print from which the reproduction originates. (Even this qualification is far from rigid; I have occasionally, and unexpectedly, had pictures reproduced bigger than the original prints — and without editorial complaint.)

When ordering enlargements from a film processing service, you should specify that they be on glossy paper (not 'silk' or 'lustre') and preferably that they be printed without white borders — ie with 'bled' edges. And we have already mentioned the advantage of marking up a contact print sheet with the boundaries of any less-than-whole-frame enlarging that you want.

Storing negatives

As you take more and more pictures to accompany your articles, you will build up a stock of potentially valuable negatives. (When you sell a photograph to a magazine, you are only selling the right to a single reproduction; you can sell the same picture over and over. This is different from the rights in your written work, for which you are — almost always — selling the right of *first* reproduction.)

You should therefore establish a system for storing your valuable negatives — so that you can retrieve the appropriate one for its next intended sale.

As a professional — or a professionally operating — photographer, you would need a system of listing and indexing every negative. As a writer-photographer you probably don't need such a sophisticated system. I have always managed well enough with a largely visual system. I use the Paterson Negative File and Visual Filing System.

I file all negatives in transparent sleeves — one complete film to a sheet. The purpose-made sheets are punched for filing in a ring-binder. Immediately above the negative sheets, I file the appropriate contact print sheet. The negative sleeve-sheet and the contact print sheet are both numbered identically, and the contact sheet is given a descriptive title of the film contents.

The numbering system I use is simple: the last two numbers of the year and then a running film number through the year. Thus, Film 90/6 is the sixth film processed in 1990. (I file colour films too and mark these with a C — thus 90/C6.) An individual negative, should I need to number it, would then be 90/6/35.

Basically though, I rely on flipping through the sheets of contacts to retrieve the negative I am looking for. I almost always have a vague picture in my mind when I go searching for a negative. And my visual search is aided by the descriptive titles on each contact sheet.

Of course, I have my 'favourite' negatives — the ones I manage to sell again and again. (The picture of my son feeding the Morris Dance dragon is an example of one such.) With these negatives, I maintain a separate list of numbers for ease and speed of reference.

And, one final piece of advice about negative filing, learnt from painful experience. Be sure to replace the negatives in their rightful places when they are returned from printing. Stray negatives get lost. And you can guarantee that the misplaced negative is the one you need next — and urgently.

(I recently made the mistake of putting a 'dragon' negative away, with some spare prints, in my dragon cuttings and research file; and then spent two days searching for it, a month or so later.)

5

PRESENTATION OF
PHOTOGRAPHS

So far, in this book, we have looked only at the production of photographs suitable to accompany a writer-photographer's articles. But having produced these top-quality, saleable photographs, how do you submit them?

As with the submission of a manuscript to an editor, so too are there specific requirements for the presentation of photographs:

- the photographs have to be captioned — and identified as yours;
- the captions have to be 'associated with the appropriate photograph;
- you have to provide a sufficiency of photographs — a choice;
- the photographs must reach the editor in perfect condition — they must therefore be properly packed.

Captions

For the avoidance of confusion, the caption is the short piece of text which accompanies a published photograph and tells what it represents. The caption for a news photograph may be slightly fuller and explain more than the caption to an article illustration; this, in turn, may be fuller than the caption for an 'artistic' picture. But they all serve the same purpose. You must use your own judgement about how full to make your caption.

The basic requirement of a caption is that it clearly provides all the information which is necessary for its purpose. Thus, a news photograph should identify name, perhaps home address, and perhaps age of the subject, an explanation of what the subject is doing, and why. It may also need to specify where and when the picture was taken. The press photographer is trained to provide the answers to the six basic newsman's questions:

who?
what?
why?
where?
when?
how?

A caption for a news-type photograph might therefore say something like:

(*who?*) Sixteen-year-old schoolgirl Denise Brightly (*what?*) cuddles her dog Patch (*why?*) who saved her from an attack by wild hedgehogs (*where?*) on her way home from school (*when?*) yesterday. (*how?*) Patch pushed the hedgehogs aside with his nose, which was badly scratched in the process.

A caption for an illustration which accompanies an article need not be so comprehensive. You can be more choosy as to which of the basic questions you answer. The text of my article about dragons (*See* Figure 3.1) included the sentence:

And the Sussex-based Chanctonbury Morris Men include a friendly dragon in their group, to the delight of their audiences. (*where? who? what? and why?*)

The caption for the photograph of my son 'feeding' that dragon needed therefore only to say:

Feeding the Chanctonbury Morris Men's dragon. (*just what?*)

An alternative approach was adopted by the editor of *TNT* magazine when captioning my photographs accompanying the article *Statues of Dissent* (Figure 3.3). In this giveaway magazine, whose readers are perhaps more prone to skim the pages, the editor chose to use a longer caption. For the statue of Oliver Cromwell, for instance, the caption read:

(*who? and what?*) The statue of Oliver Cromwell, the Lord Protector, which stands (*where?*) inside the grounds of the Palace of Westminster, (*why?*) looking out onto Parliament Square.

The important thing about a caption is, to repeat, that it provide *sufficient* information — and, in the case of an article illustration, that it relates to the article. And always, you will find that it helps, to keep in the back of your mind, the newsman's six basic questions.

There is one further point to bear in mind. You never know which of your several submitted photographs the editor will choose to use. While the captions may therefore acceptably relate back to the text of the article, the article itself should never refer to specific pictures which may or may not be chosen. The only exception to this is when the whole article stands or falls on the presence of a particular photograph — in which case, the editor should be advised of the need for this picture's inclusion. Acceptance of your illustrated feature article may then depend on the quality and general acceptability of the essential illustration. It's a big risk.

The caption written — or at least, its content decided — we need to consider how it is to be physically associated with the relevant picture. There are two (and a half) ways of associating captions with pictures.

In all cases, the caption must be typed, preferably double-spaced. One approach is then for the slip of paper with the caption typed on it to be cut from the 'parent' A4 sheet and fixed to the *back* of the picture. (Never use ordinary glue to fix anything to the back of a photograph. I fix my caption slips, when necessary, with strips of Cellotape, just at the ends.) Each caption slip should also carry a key word from the article title — so that pictures and text can be associated — and the name of the writer-photographer. Something like:

Dragons/Wells
Feeding the Chanctonbury Morris Men's dragon.

Another very similar way of captioning, (the 'half' mentioned above) is for a rather larger piece of paper, with the same wording, to be fixed to the bottom edge of the back of the print, facing forward. In this way, the caption hangs below the picture and is readable from the front. For packing, the dangling caption has then to be folded forward, over the print. This is an approach favoured by PR firms; I have never used it.

My normal approach to captioning is to provide a separate sheet of captions. This standard A4 sheet is packed with the manuscript. It is headed with the article title in full, my name in full, and the sub-heading CAPTIONS. Then follows each of the several captions; these are exactly as before except that each one is now given a key letter — but not the title or name 'keys'. Thus:

A   Feeding   the   Chanctonbury   Morris   Men's
     dragon.

Of course, this second approach also entails marking the back of every associated picture with the relevant key letter. And you need to be very careful when marking the back of any photograph.

You must take particular care not to mark the back of any photograph with a hard pen or pencil. If you do, assuredly the marks will show through on the face of the photograph, rendering it potentially unusable. At the same time, the plastic-coated paper on which some enlargements are made, will not accept felt-tip pen ink — it will not dry and smudges on contact with other papers. You need to experiment and check. My personal approach is to use a very soft pencil. And I try to make my marks behind a dark area on the front of the picture, where they are less likely to show through. For the dragon feeding picture then, I would merely write on the back, lightly, in soft pencil:

Dragons (A)

Whichever method used for captioning the pictures, you also need to identify yourself and your address. The small adhesive address labels widely advertised in newspapers are ideal for this purpose. Fix the label in a remote corner of the print — not slap bang in the middle.

Editorial choice

The photographs captioned and identified, how many do you send? You are supplying photographs *with an article* — NOT as a portfolio of pictures for editorial retention and occasional use. So, you don't want to send too many (think of the cost of postage); at the same time, there must be enough — you don't want the editor to bring in extra pictures from elsewhere.

As with most matters relating to selling illustrated feature articles to magazines, the question is best resolved by market study. Study similar illustrated articles in the 'target' magazine; note how many illustrations are normally used. If articles are usually accompanied by say three illustrations, offer the editor five — six at the absolute outside. (And, in Chapter 3, we looked at the balance of upright and landscape pictures. Try to offer a similar balance.)

Try also to offer the editor a selection of *types* of photograph. Offer close-ups and street scenes, landscapes and people doing something. Don't offer all street scenes or all people working. Offer a variety.

Presentation and packing

The photographs are selected, captioned and emblazoned with your name and address sticker; the article is written. (More about that below, but for now, assume it is written.) What now?

As with any unsolicited feature article, it is my belief (and practice) that a brief covering letter is necessary. This would say something like:

Dear Mr Bloggs

I enclose herewith, for your consideration for publication in *Widget-keepers Weekly*, at your usual rates of payment, a thousand-word article entitled 'The Fidgety Widgets of Ancient Andorra'. The article is illustrated with five black and white photographs — all taken by myself.

If you use the illustrated article, I would appreciate, in addition to payment, a voucher copy of the issue of *Widget-keepers Weekly* in which it appears. If the material is not of interest, I would appreciate its return, for which purpose I enclose the customary stamped addressed envelope.

Yours sincerely

Gerry Attrick

If you are using 7″ × 5″ photographs, the whole package can fit into a C5 (9″ × 6⅜″) envelope. Fold the article manuscript, caption sheet and covering letter neatly in half. You also need, as referred to above, a return envelope; clearly this needs to be the same size as the despatch envelope. Address it, stamp it (the same as for despatch) and fold it in two.

Next, find a piece of thin (but not too thin) card and cut it to about 8½″ × 6″ – bigger than the 7″ × 5″ prints yet small enough to fit inside the envelope. Place the photographs with the pictures facing the card.

Put the folded article, letter, return envelope, etc. on the picture side of the package of photographs. Now stretch an elastic band across opposite corners to hold it all in place — and insert the whole in the despatch envelope. Put it in the envelope so that the pictures and the article are at the back and the card on the address side. This way, the card will take the pressure of the postmark imprint — and the photographs will not be damaged even if someone stamps the back too.

(It will be appreciated from the above just how essential a letter balance is to a writer-photographer. Only by knowing the weight of the manuscript and picture (plus protective card) package can the return envelope be adequately prepaid without a double trip to the Post Office. Most unillustrated articles come within the limit of the 'basic' 60g postage; illustrated articles never do.)

If you have decided that you need to supply 10″ × 8″ photographs — perhaps because of the 'quality' of the target magazine and/or its habitual use of large photo-spreads — you will clearly need a bigger envelope. You must, of course, never fold a photograph — if folded, it is ruined; nor must it be so little protected that the postman can readily fold it. (Some postmen seem to delight in folding all large envelopes before pushing them through amply large letter-boxes.)

With the larger envelope (C4 = 12¾″ × 9″) you will need stronger card than with the C5 one — it is far more likely to be folded. You no longer need to fold the article and covering letter. (But, of course, the return envelope — again C4 — must still be folded in order to fit inside the despatch envelope.) Other than that, the packing process should be identical.

One final proviso: if your manuscript itself is long — say two thousand five hundred words or more — it is better not to fold it at all. Then, even if you are only supplying 7″ × 5″ photographs, you will still use a C4 envelope — and an A4-sized protective card.

Figure 5.1 shows the packaging of a typical illustrated article.

The accompanying article

As explained at the start, this book is directed at writers who wish to illustrate their work with simple photographs. Undoubtedly though, some readers will be more adept than others at the craft of writing articles. The best course of action for the less expert would be to buy a copy of my earlier book, *The Craft of Writing Articles* (Allison & Busby), which deals specifically with the writing process. But it may help them — and perhaps act as a 'revision course' for others — to run briefly through the article-writing process.

There are four parts to the article-writing business: the writing itself is only one of these four. The four elements are:

Fig. 5.1

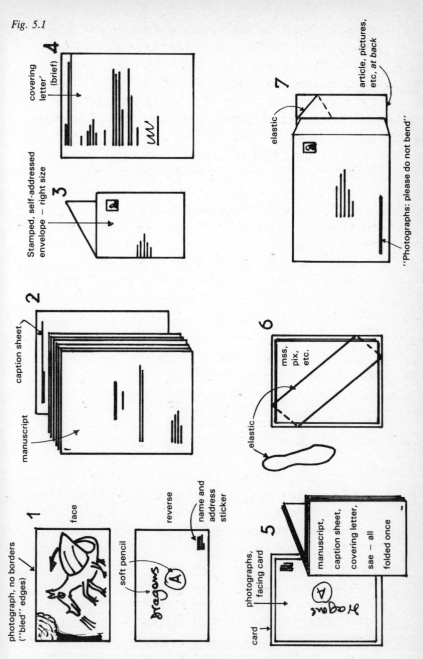

The packaging of an illustrated article ready for submission, on spec, *to an Editor.*

- getting the idea — deciding what you are going to write about
- studying and selecting the market
- writing the article
- presenting and selling the article.

And getting the idea for the article is, if not the most important, at least the 'first among equals'.

What to write about

An article-writer is, first and foremost, an ideas person. If you have no ideas for articles, you can't write them. An idea is to an article-writer what petrol is to a car; without it, you're stuck.

So, you must get yourself an idea for this (illustrated) article you are intending to write. And the first basic advice given in every writing book, and to every beginning writer, is:

WRITE ABOUT WHAT YOU KNOW

This is excellent — if perhaps somewhat limiting — advice. (You will rapidly grow out of it, if you interpret it too literally. As you develop as a writer though, you will find that you will continually increase 'what you know' about). But let's start from there.

'Write about what you know.' Fine. What do you know about? 'Not a lot,' I hear you say. But you are wrong. We all have a wealth of personal experiences, of knowledge about our job or hobby, or knowledge about some small thing that interests us. And as a writer you can build on this. Let's look more closely at this. I believe that everyone 'knows' about — and can often go on to write about:

- their job or hobby
- their personal experiences
- their particular interest

Whatever your job or hobby, it is likely that you know quite a lot about at least some small part of it. (As an example, using my own work experience, I sold two articles on how to answer the telephone. Any working person could have written these — but I thought of, and developed, the idea.)

Maybe your hobby is coin collecting, or growing *bonsai* trees, or keeping pet arachnids. You can write an article — indeed, several articles — about any of these hobbies. And many others too.

Do you work as a carpenter, or a tiler, or an accountant, or a secretary? There are articles to be written about any of these occupations. (And about any other occupation too.) The carpenter, for instance, could write about how to repair a broken chair or replace a rotted window-sill; the tiler about how to replace *one* cracked tile without breaking others; the accountant about the simplest way of completing a VAT return; and the secretary, perhaps about how to manage a boss. (I once sold an article about how to work with a secretary. But the magazine 'folded' — and I never did get paid for it.)

The job/hobby opportunities for articles are almost limitless. The hobby articles will tend to be those most suited to illustration. A set of photographs of interesting items from your coin collection would be an excellent basis for an illustrated article. So too would pictures of *bonsai* trees at various stages. Or how to transplant them. And so on.

Personal experiences are another fruitful area for article ideas. And within this general heading I would include nostalgic reminiscences, travel advice, everyday domestic activities, success stories, self-healing or other health advice, or anything *really* unusual or interesting.

The most important thing to remember in experience-based articles is to ensure that they help or interest the reader. Don't write about your own holiday; write about how the reader can enjoy a similar one — by following in your footsteps. What you said to Aunt Mabel may interest or amuse you and perhaps Aunt Mabel; it's very doubtful if it will be of interest to anyone else.

And articles on personal experiences need not be restricted to your own activities. If a friend or neighbour does something interesting or unusual, you can write about that. The friendly neighbour will usually be only too happy to tell you all about it. All you have to do is write it up — professionally.

Personal experience articles — particularly travel ones — are very suitable for illustrating. Always take pictures of the unusual, the interesting, the person doing something. Picture things and activities to which the reader can relate.

The third of the areas about which most people have knowledge is 'the special interest'. This may be something connected with work and therefore already covered above. But there is also the person who is fascinated by how lace is made, or by stories of Britain's (original) Industrial Revolution, or Greek history or . . . — and has read a lot about it. That person has made themselves a 'mini-expert' on their special interest. And that person could probably write about it.

(For example — I am fascinated by dragons: I have collected lots of information about dragons; and now, over the years, I have sold several illustrated articles about dragons. *See* Chapter 3. You can do the same. I recently met again someone whom earlier, I had similarly advised: she is now a 'mini-expert' on garden gnomes. I look forward to seeing her gnome articles in print.)

As you develop as a writer-photographer, you will find that you extend your interests; you become a mini-expert in more fields. And then, you have more topics on which to 'write about what you know'.

But enough of ideas and subjects. The best article ideas are those that relate to a specific market for your work.

Market study

You cannot, with any hope of success, write — and illustrate — an article . . . and then think about where to submit it. Each of the magazines fighting for survival on the crowded shelves of station bookstalls differs from its competitors. Each magazine has a different readership and caters for it in its own individual way. If you are to sell your work to magazines, you must *know* their specific requirements. And meet them.

How are you to ascertain the requirements of the different magazines? By studying them. But to study them all is a huge task. So you must reduce the number of magazine which you plan to 'attack'.

Think first about the magazines that you already know well. If your hobby is collecting coins, you have probably been subscribing to *Coin Monthly* for years. You *are* the typical reader. You *know* the policies, the interests, the requirements of at least the current editor. (But take care. Editors change jobs quite frequently — and often, the magazine's policy changes with them.) This magazine must be a sensible one for you to try writing for.

The same principles apply if you have subscribed for years to *The Lady*, or *Good Housekeeping*, or *Do It Yourself*. These should be your first 'targets'.

But in time, even if not initially, you will also wish to write for other markets. Perhaps you want to write a general-interest article about your specialist interest; the specialist magazine will not be interested in this — you need to identify a new market.

The first source of information about further, general-interest markets will be one of the writers' market reference books. The long-established (for more than eighty years) *Writers' & Artists' Yearbook* (A & C Black) is one such; its very comprehensiveness is its only real defect. It lists so many magazines (and book publishers, and agents, and radio and TV companies, and . . .) that a reader is overwhelmed — and inevitably offered only minimal information.

My own, frequently updated book *The Magazine Writers' Handbook* (Allison & Busby) gets round this problem. It reviews a relatively small number (seventy plus) of carefully selected, general-interest magazines in considerable detail. For each: it looks at the subjects of recent articles and stories; it identifies the areas in which the magazine has its own 'resident' experts; it also advises on individual submission requirements, how long decisions usually take, likely payments, etc.

But no reference book can do all your market study for you. Even my own can only 'take off the rough

116

edges' for you — help you narrow down the choice of which magazine you choose to study further. You must still do your own detailed study of any new-to-you 'target magazine'.

Ideally, to assist you in targetting the submission of your illustrated article, you should look in the magazine for a published article of a similar type to the one you wish to submit. Another personal experience article, or another on a general-interest subject.

If you can find a broadly similar article, study it in detail. Count the words: overall and in the longest and shortest sentences and paragraphs. Note the use, or otherwise, of anecdotes; study how the article is put together — is there a logical sequence? Does the magazine perhaps prefer a, 'bitty' style — lots of short 'boxed' snippets of information connected by a common topic?

You need this information for when you come to write your own. The article you are studying was acceptable to the editor. You can usefully model your own first article on it. Not word for word of course, but you should work to a similar overall length, made up of about the same number of similarly varied paragraphs; and if the model uses few or many anecdotes, so too should yours. You need to inform yourself about the number and type of accompanying illustrations too. (*See* Editorial choice, above.)

Writing the article

Market study completed, you should now know which magazine you are going to write for; you believe too, that your idea is suitable for that choice of magazine. And as part of the development of the idea, you know *what* you are going to say in your article. You are now ready to start the actual writing.

Put aside your fears. Writing an article — and particularly an illustrated article — is NOT a bit like writing a composition or essay at school. If you can talk over the garden fence to your neighbour about your hobby or interest, you can write an article. You don't need to be a literary genius — indeed, that could easily be a real handicap.

First, list the things you are going to *say* in your article. If it is about replacing a tile, list the steps in the process. If it is about the history of Tasmahalian paper-money, list the major events and different types. If it is about holidaying under canvas on Wandsworth Common, list the key points in its favour.

Now review the points you have listed and think about the most interesting sequence in which to present them. You need to start with a 'bang' — to grab the reader's interest; at the same time you need to make sure you don't end with a whimper — you need a 'bang' there too. And you mustn't let it sag in the middle either.

The more time you spend on thinking about the sequence and the *impact* of different parts of the article, the better the final result will be. Once you know what you are going to say where, the actual writing will be that much easier.

When your contents are listed and 'sequenced', you are ready to start writing 'joined-up words'.

The next thing to think about is the need of the reader. As a writer-photographer you are in the entertainment business. You need to interest and entertain the reader. The moment the reader becomes bored, or finds your writing hard to understand, you've failed. You've lost the reader. (And the editor — who makes

118

the decision on whether or not to buy your article and photographs — knows just what will, and what will not, please the magazine readership. That's an editor's job.)

Your task is to *communicate* directly with that reader. You must never seek to impress that reader with your personal knowledge, skill, or importance. Indeed, the more you can make yourself 'invisible' or 'transparent' — un-noticeable — the better your writing is.

The best way of communicating 'transparently' is to write as clearly and as simply as you possibly can.

Clear, simple writing comes largely from the use of:

- short, simple words
- short sentences — and simple punctuation
- short-looking paragraphs

and from seeking to:

- 'write as you talk'.

(That last recommendation comes from the American management and writing *guru*, Robert Gunning. It can be better — but far less succinctly — put, as: 'write in a way that you would not find uncomfortable to read aloud'. You can test that.)

First, simple words. If, when reading, you come across a word you don't know, your immediate reaction is to read on, assuming that its meaning will come clear from its context. If it doesn't, as likely as not, you will still just read on, but feeling slightly peeved. If this happens frequently within an article, you will become increasingly disenchanted. The average reader will probably have given up long before. (The average

119

reader — less fond of 'words' than the writer-photographer — is also less likely to consult a dictionary.)

Simple words tend to be short words. So, before you use a long word, ask yourself whether two or three short words wouldn't be easier to understand. We usually use long words more to impress than to communicate. And our job is not to impress. Not ever.

Next, short sentences. You should have determined, from your study of the article you selected as a 'model', how short most published sentences are. Not that there is anything fundamentally wrong with a long sentence. But it is difficult to write an easily-understood long sentence, whereas short sentences are almost always easy to understand.

Count your words as you write. (The author, John Braine, once wrote, 'a writer is a person who counts words.') Count other people's words too. Most popular, general-interest magazines use short sentences. Most untrained writers write long sentences. And most badly-written long sentences contain an 'and' in the middle. Often, that 'and' can be better replaced with a full stop and a capital letter. Such a change will almost invariably improve the ease of understanding of the resultant two sentences. (Or you can retain the 'And' to improve the 'flow'.)

In general, I write to an average sentence length of about sixteen words, and a maximum length of twenty-five. I don't stick rigidly to these figures — occasionally I go 'over the top' — but they are a good yardstick. I recommend that you work to the same target figures. They make the reading easy. And that's what it's all about.

If you confine yourself — largely — to writing in short sentences, with a maximum length of twenty-five words, punctuating them becomes easy. Full stops and commas will generally suffice. And that is good simple punctuation.

Colons and semi-colons are, of course, useful. But it is not always easy to be sure when to use what. The easy way out is to avoid using them until you are more skilled. Broadly though, use a semi-colon instead of a full stop, where you want to link two associated thoughts together. Use a colon only to introduce a list — and don't use the old-fashioned colon-and-a-dash at all. (A colon has another use — with two 'balanced' thoughts — but this need not concern us.)

Avoid altogether using the exclamation mark in feature articles. It is usually the sign of an amateur writer who cannot convey surprise or emphasis with mere words. Similarly with underlining. Leave this to 'Disgusted, Tunbridge Wells'; a writer should be able to emphasise by the choice of words alone. (To the printer, underlining means 'print in italics' — and, to me, italics do not usually look particularly emphatic.)

Stick to full stops and commas. Remember that the purpose of punctuation is to make the writing easier to understand. And as a general rule, use less punctuation rather than more. Under-punctuate wherever possible.

The reason for recommending the use of short paragraphs is not quite the same as for short sentences. It is the appearance of the paragraph length that is most important, rather than its actual length. A long paragraph looks as though it will be 'difficult'; a short paragraph looks easy. So . . . in narrow newspaper-like columns of print, the actual paragraph length needs to be short; conversely, in a wide, magazine column, a paragraph containing the same number of words would look ridiculously short.

As a very general rule, for magazine articles, try to work to an average paragraph length of about sixty words — and a maximum of about eighty. (And an opening paragraph will always be improved — have more 'impact' — if held down to about half the average length.)

With both sentences and paragraphs though, do not let the above advice make your writing become too standardised. As far as possible within the average and maximum recommended lengths, ensure that the lengths of individual sentences and paragraphs vary. All short sentences will *feel* staccato and urgent. Long sentences *feel* slow. If all your paragraphs are of much the same length the writing will look dull. Vary the lengths.

Polishing

The advice of Robert Gunning (cited above) is particularly appropriate when it comes to revising and polishing your writing. You should, throughout, have been striving to make your writing simple; to use words and phrases that you would not find difficult to read aloud.

No matter how hard we strive to write simply though, ALL writers occasionally over-write, waffle, or include the odd pompous phrase just because it 'looks good'. The successful writer is the writer who goes back over his/her work and polishes it.

Polishing means cutting out all the over-writing, and the pomposities. Polishing means tightening up your writing.

One of the best ways of identifying the waffle is to read your work aloud. The pompous phrase, the unnecessary word, the over-long sentence, will all become obvious. Read them, identify them — and cut them out. And when you find a phrase or sentence with the construction or expression of which you are particularly pleased — cross that out too. Rewrite it, more simply.

While reading your work through, think also about the flow, particularly from paragraph to paragraph. Try to start each paragraph with a phrase which links it back to the one before. (As a last resort, start the next paragraph with an 'And'. But don't do this too often.) Paragraphs should contain separate thoughts — but consecutive thoughts should follow a logical sequence. Too many unlinked paragraphs suggest a butterfly mind rather than that of an expert writer.

Presentation

Your article is now written — and nicely polished. The accompanying photographs are printed, captioned and ready for despatch. All that remains is to prepare the article itself for despatch. You cannot submit it in long-hand.

The presentation of an article manuscript is very important. There is only one right way of submitting it. An article manuscript must:

- by typed, double-spaced (ie, type a line, miss a line) — using any standard typeface; (avoid for instance, typewriters that produce mock hand-writing or only large and small capital letters.)
- be on white A4 paper — of reasonable thickness; (use 70 gsm or 80 gsm paper — gsm being grammes per square metre, the weight of the paper.)
- have large margins — 40–50 mm on left and at least 25 mm at top, bottom, and right;

- have a constant (5-space) indent at the start of each paragraph; (but usually, not the first paragraph.)
- have numbered — and identified — pages; (provide a 'strap' at top right corner of each page, giving your name, a key word from the title, and the page number.)
- have — at least, in my view it's a must — a cover sheet stating title, author, number of words (to nearest hundred — NOT precisely, that's amateurish), number of accompanying photographs, and writer-photographer's address;
- have, on the last page, of the manuscript, the word 'END' and, beneath that, the writer-photographer's name and address again.

That's it. That's article writing and presentation in the proverbial nutshell. Just remember that you are in the entertainment business. You are NOT writing for posterity. (If you want to learn more about the writing process, get a copy of my book, *The Craft of Writing Articles*, Allison & Busby.)

A final word of advice: always keep a copy of all your typed manuscripts. Once in a few years a manuscript goes astray — and it'd be a pity to waste all that hard work. More importantly, it is very useful to compare your text with the final published version. To see how an editor changes your words is the best tuition available.

6

BUSINESS MATTERS

The writer-photographer is 'in business'. The objective — in no matter how small a way — is to *sell* packages of words and pictures. If nothing else, payment is the measure of the success or otherwise of the writer-photographer. But merely by adding photography to the writing business, the writer-photographer's expenses have been significantly increased. It behoves the keen freelancer to strive to recoup that expense – many-fold.

There are several aspects of the business which need to be remarked upon. And adding photography to the writing business means one or two changes in attitudes and expectations. We need specifically to think about:

- rights
- agents
- competitions
- markets other than accompanying articles

- likely remuneration
- necessary records
- generally being business-like

Rights

When you write an article, and submit it to a specific magazine, you are implicitly offering First British Serial Rights. That is, the selected magazine may buy the right to use the article once, on the understanding that it has not previously been published.

(Short story writers, who can perhaps sell the same story, unaltered, to other magazines, always specify first British Serial Rights — FBSR — on the cover sheet. And this is wise — for them.)

Sometimes a magazine will ask for World, or other Rights in an article. I will almost always agree to sell them whatever rights they want. For this reason, I see no purpose in specifying the offered rights in an article; it is unlikely that the same 'literary' approach would be appropriate to any other magazine. And at any time, I can always use the same facts in a further rewritten, re-slanted article for another magazine, irrespective of the rights the magazine buys. But this is for later.

Remember: there is no copyright in facts — only in the way in which they are presented. In other words, you can rewrite virtually any article in several different ways, from a single set of facts.

(Ideally, you will not use all of your facts in any one article. In this way you are ensuring a partially different content to any subsequent article. As well as a different way of writing them up.)

The reason for mentioning the rights in written work

is to compare this with the rights you will be offering in your black and white photographs. So long as you have taken the photographs yourself, in public places, of consenting (or at least non-objecting) people, and not while working on commission for a client, then the copyright in your pictures is yours.

It was necessary to be pedantic about that statement. You cannot photograph people in non-public places — eg their home — if they object. (You cannot photograph a person even in a public place and then use that photograph for advertising purposes either — without a specific 'release'.) And if you photograph something or someone while employed for the purpose, then the copyright in the photographs will usually belong to your client/employer.

However, given that the copyright in your pictures is yours, you can offer them for sale. When you submit a photographic print (ie enlargement) to a magazine, you are offering the editor no more than the right to use the picture for a single reproduction. There is no need to specify this, it is implied by custom. The editor may buy World Rights in the article and sell it on to a foreign editor; the editor cannot similarly sell the picture — a further reproduction fee must be paid.

An editor could justifiably be annoyed if an identical article appeared in his/her, and in another, magazine at around the same time. He/she has bought *First* rights. But he has no right (sorry) to feel peeved at seeing an identical photograph repeated elsewhere.

(Furthermore, although the facts are free-for-all, it would not be politic for *you* to provide a competing magazine with even a broadly similar article for several months after the first sale.)

On occasions, inexperienced editors — usually of small magazines — may seek to buy 'All Rights' in a photograph. You should almost always refuse. They will always give in; if not, walk away. (Or a big editor might just make you an offer you couldn't refuse — for a really spectacular shot. And even then, *see below* about taking more than one picture of just about everything.)

Just about every writer-photographer worth their salt can point to photographs that have sold over and over again. I have, for example, sold the picture of my son feeding the Chanctonbury dragon about half a dozen times — and will undoubtedly sell it again.

You do not need to tell an editor that a picture has been sold before. This is no concern of the editor's. (By contrast, if you are trying — and you'll need a lot of luck — to sell Second British Serial Rights in an unchanged article, you *must* tell the editor about its previous publication.)

Picture agencies

Literary agents are not usually of interest or importance to the 'ordinary' article-writer: an agent would not normally be interested in taking on such a client. (If you are a successful novelist and are asked to write a series of feature articles, you would probably already have an agent, who would then handle the articles — charging you the standard literary agents' 10 or 15 per cent commission. But not otherwise: if not a novelist, you probably have no agent.)

Equally, a photographer who sells only a few pictures, largely *on spec*, will not be of interest to a picture agency. Nor will an 'ordinary' writer-photographer.

A typical picture agency will want to handle a large batch of pictures from any photographer it takes on.

Many ask for a minimum submission of 500 pictures to look at when considering whether or not to handle your work; a submission of 100 black and white pictures is the least requirement of almost any agency. (But *see* next chapter: colour pictures for use in travel brochures.)

A typical picture agency commission is 50 per cent. But they do sell the pictures again and again, and probably at far better rates than you could achieve yourself. A good agency does an awful lot of hard work for its 50 per cent.

Realistically though, the 'ordinary' writer-photographer need not bother with picture agencies. (And, as a *quid pro quo*, the picture agencies in turn, will not bother themselves with the writer-photographer.)

Competitions

There are very few competitions for 'ordinary' article-writers. What few there are, usually are restricted to competitions run by writing circles for their members, and for members of other writing circles. And the prizes are small. (By comparison — and as a largely irrelevant aside — poetry, for which the 'ordinary' market is minimal, has several, major, open competitions with really huge prizes.)

But — as we have already mentioned in Chapter 3 — competitions are very important to the small-time photographer. (And the 'ordinary' writer-photographer undoubtedly falls into this category too.) Every year there are lots of photographic competitions, open to all, and offering very attractive prizes. The 'ordinary' writer-photographer would be foolish to pass up these opportunities.

Fig. 6.1

A competition-winning photograph of mine. Note the strong, simple, composition and the lack of extraneous detail. The competition was in a major overseas newspaper.

Most of the more popular photographic magazines run frequent small competitions and often a major annual one too. For these competitions, you need to watch the relevant magazines. Figure 6.1 is a competition-winning photograph of mine; the competition was in a major overseas newspaper.

But there are other photo competitions too. A recent competition, run by a wool firm, offered a small car for the first prize and five second prizes of £100 each. Another, run by a whisky distiller, offered two round-the-world air tickets plus expenses, worth £5000 for first prize — and £500 each for ten runners-up. And only a month or so earlier, Kodak ran a 'Find Your Local Hero' competition: they asked for a photograph

130

demonstrating the hero's activity — and offered a first prize of a holiday in Thailand for the photographer, and £500 for the hero.

Competitions such as those mentioned above are always being announced.

(Many are listed — and this is my source for the above mentions — in the well-established monthly *Freelance Market News* (previously known as the *Contributor's Bulletin*). This is well worth any freelance writer-photographer subscribing to: not just for competitions, it reports regularly on many new — and changed old — markets for illustrated articles. It is published by Freelance Press Services, Cumberland House, Lissadell Street, Salford, Manchester M6 6GG. Currently, an 11-issue annual subscription costs £18.50.)

As a sweeping generalisation, most non-specialist photographic competitions look for entries showing people. Preferably happy people. Preferably people doing something — and certainly not just looking at the camera. And often, preferably children — with or without animals. So . . . ALWAYS be on the look-out for potential competition material. (Which means, to reiterate, having a camera handy at all times.)

Many competitions are open to both professional and amateur photographers. Initially, it might be wise to avoid those in which professionals can compete. Being an 'ordinary' writer-photographer does not make you a 'pro'. Many competitions too, have two categories. One for black and white pictures and another for colour prints. (*See* Chapter 7 for advice on colour photography.) Unless the rules preclude it, submit in both categories. The black and white competition, from 'non-pros', is likely to be limited.

Watch out, particularly, for the smaller competitions. Thousands of photographers will enter the bigger contests; your chances will be correspondingly reduced. Smaller prizes mean less competition, ie more chance for you. And even the smallest first prize is very sweet.

A few further (and slightly repetitive) words of general advice about entering photographic competitions may help:

- Read the rules. Comply with them. Most people don't bother. If you do, you immediately lift yourself out of 'the ruck'. The sort of thing often ignored is a maximum print size, a requirement for a glossy finish, the need for an entry form or a product label, or just a closing date.
- Go for size. Having read the rules, always submit the biggest print (or colour transparency) permitted. If you don't, someone else will — and the bigger the picture the more *impact* it has.
- Go for quality. Never submit anything less than your very best — and ensure that your very best is of an extremely high quality. If you don't submit your very best, someone else will. And theirs will be better than yours. A lot of rubbish is inevitably submitted to every competition. A good quality entry automatically stands out.
- Be different — but not too different. The judges of any contest are usually bored stiff as they wade through the huge number of extremely poor entries. They will delight in finding something just that little bit better. If you can surprise, and interest — or even better still, amuse — them, you will have a good head start on the rest. If the competition has a theme, strive to find an unusual way of interpreting it. At the same time though,

132

beware of 'bending' one of your filed negatives to 'fit' the contest rules. Make your originality a positive effort.

- Be prepared to lose the copyright in a winning entry. And the way to be prepared is to take several similar — but not quite identical — shots of the same potentially prize-winning picture. This way, you can happily sacrifice the copyright in ONE NEGATIVE ONLY while preserving the right to sell similar ones elsewhere.

  Beware though — and do not enter for — any competition which requires the sacrifice of the copyright of *all* entries. This requirement is quite iniquitous; the competition organisers get a lot of potentially very good quality material for free.

Other markets

So far, we have only considered using your photographs as illustrations to articles (or 'Letters'), or in competitions. But there may be other markets.

It used to be possible to sell your photographs for use as picture postcards or in calendars. But in recent years these markets have turned over — almost exclusively — to colour. You might find a picture postcard publisher who was interested in the odd black and white picture — but you'd have to look very hard to find them. It would be even harder to find a calendar publisher interested in a black and white picture today.

Book publishers however, still use a lot of black and white pictures as internal illustrations (ie, as opposed to the book covers). But they will usually go to picture agencies for their requirements. Your only chance here is to be 'known' as a supplier of black and white pic-

133

tures of a particular specialism. Then, publishers (and authors) will beat a path to your door.

In summary then, the market for black and white photographs is almost exclusively the general-interest magazines plus a few newspapers. (But that is still a relatively big market.)

Remuneration

If you — a writer — are going to make the transition into a writer-photographer, you will wish to assure yourself that it is financially worth the effort. In a nutshell, it is.

On average — ie from the small low-paying magazine to the higher-paying specialist magazine — I estimate that I am paid about £50 to £60 per thousand words for my written work. (Of course, to earn that on average, it means that some of my features sell for £100 a thousand words and some for only £20.) That translates very roughly into about £50 per magazine page.

If I sell photographs as part of the 'package', they are usually reproduced at just less than quarter-page size — say, one-fifth-page size. And, on average, I get paid about £10 to £12 per picture. The words and the pictures therefore attract about the same remuneration.

If I wish to sell the words again, I must rewrite them. If I wish to sell the picture again, I just resubmit it — which entails less extra work. (I may, of course, have to pay for a new print being made. Quite a lot of magazines though, return the photographic prints after they have been used. They can then be re-used.)

At the very least therefore, selling pictures with the words is worth the effort because:

- it increases your chances of selling — because you are offering an editor an attractive, complete and ready-made, 'package';
- (usually) you get paid at least the same page-rate for pictures as for words — and really, once you get used to it, the work in producing the pictures is considerably less than the work in writing the words;
- you can often resell the pictures — again and again — without more ado.

If you get a commission to produce words and pictures — or even just pictures — for a magazine feature, you will be paid more than the lowish average rate I have quoted above. (And for colour — *see* next chapter — you will be paid considerably more.)

Records

As we have already remarked, every writer-photographer is 'in business'. And this means that he/she will wish (and in some cases, need) to keep certain records.

I suggest that you need to keep records of:

- picture subjects — filed, as we have already discussed, in a visual filing system;
- articles written and submitted — to which magazine, and with which illustrations (you need to ensure you do not send the same, or a similar, feature to the same magazine twice – nor, too soon, to a competitor);
- articles and pictures sold — and for how much (it is interesting but not really essential, to record the earnings of individual negatives — I don't bother);

- earnings in a business year — and, alongside this, all expenses in the same period.

We have already discussed the negative filing system — in Chapter 4. Now, briefly, the other records.

I keep my own records in a relatively simple system. (I believe in everything being as simple as possible. I am a writer-photographer — not an accountant or archivist.)

For my record of work submitted I maintain two A4 sheets for each year's work. The first records output: it has vertical columns headed:

Article number. (I number all my output with a single unique five-digit number: the first three digits describe the year — thus, 890 means all work done in financial yar 89/90. 901 means work produced in 90/91. The next two digits are merely a running count: 01 being the first article written in the year. Thus 89002 is the second article written in year 89/90. To date, I have never written more than 99 articles in any one year.)

File name and disk. (I write all my work on my word processor. All articles are filed with title commencing with A, followed by a few letters representing the article title. And, because my work is filed on 5¼″ 'floppy disks', I need to record the disk number so that I can retrieve the file if necessary. Thus, an article on polishing written work which is stored on disk 21 is listed as APOLISH.21.)

Title. (This is what it says — but sometimes abbreviated.)

There are then several columns under the general title of:

To/date. (Here, I record an abbreviated magazine name and the date of my submitting the article. Thus WM 21/2/90 would be an article submitted to *Writers' Monthly* on that date.
If the article is accepted by the first magazine to which it is sent, then the next column contains a square *blob* (for speed of identification of accepted work) and the letters A — C — P which are put in when: A — accepted, C — copy of published work received, and P — paid.

The final column of the sheet is headed:

Paid. (Here, I record the total payment received for the feature. I usually pencil in the payment I expect, before I get it. But this pencilling in is not part of *the system*.)

My second annual A4 sheet records 'work out' and repeats much of what is on the first sheet — but I find it convenient to maintain both. The titles of the vertical columns on the second sheet — and their purpose — are:

Number. (As above)

File. (As above)

Title. (As above)

Words/pix. (An additional column largely for my interest. It contains what it says: the number of words and the number of pictures. Thus, 800/3 indicates an 800-word article accompanied by 3 illustrations.)

137

Magazine. (What it says.)

Date submitted. (In fact, to save space this column is often merely headed 'Sent'. I simply record the date.)

Accepted/rejected — Date. (An A for an acceptance and an R for a rejection and the date at which I was so informed. I also ring the A to make it stand out more. And a record of the advice date allows me to build up a 'feel' for how long different magazines take to respond.)

Publication date. (Again, I like to develop a 'feel' for how long after work is accepted it is published.)

Paid/date. (I record the payment received — and the date I get it — again, for my overall 'feel' for the market.)

From this annual sheet I can quickly see — by glancing down the 'Accepted/rejected' column — which submissions are still awaiting decisions. And, eventually, I can collate useful information on editorial performances.

My final record is the financial one. Both for my own information and in order that I can satisfy the Inspector of Taxes, I keep a careful record of all receipts from my writer-photographer activities — and of all my expenses.

I use a multi-columned account book with the following column headings:

- Date
- Item
- Receipt code (A = articles, B = books, etc.)

- Receipts
- Expenditure

The expenditure is then repeated in subsequent columns, broken down — for ease of year-end accounting — by type:

- Post
- Research
- Stationery (including all films and processing)
- Travel (I 'charge' civil service car mileage rates)
- Telephone (I estimate the cost of all non-local calls)
- Others

Then, merely because I am interested in which aspects of my writing and associated activities are the most profitable (and cost-effective), I do a second breakdown of the expenditure figures, by activity:

- Lecturing (ie one-off talks or my one-day courses)
- Articles (including photographs)
- Books
- General running costs (and this always ends up being the most used column)

The accounting system outlined above helps me to meet the requirements of the Inspector of Taxes (I am not registered for VAT — if I were, the system needs a little expansion) and at the same time, to keep a check on what is, and what is not, cost-effective. I commend some such system to any writer-photographer.

Being business-like

Finally in this chapter, another reminder that as a writer-photographer, you are 'in business'. The more business-like and 'professional' you are — or appear to be — in all your activities, the more successful you will be.

As a writer-photographer, you are operating in a world of professional editors and professional publishers; many of your competitors will be full-time professional writers and photographers. To compete, you must work to their standards. Amateurs don't make the grade. We have looked at the writing and photography side of professionalism — that's what this book has been about — but you must also be professional in your business activities.

Being business-like need mean little more than: never missing editorial deadlines; maintaining high standards of quality; keeping your promises; using appropriate stationery; and sending out bills as necessary. The first few items in that description of perfection need no further elaboration. (Just abide by them.) But a few words about appropriate stationery etc. may be useful.

A writer-photographer needs to have headed notepaper. (The same paper can be used for invoicing, *see* below.) The paper should be of good quality: your letters are your shop-window, your ambassadors to the editorial court. Cheap stationery suggests a cheap-jack and possibly unreliable operation. An 80 gsm bond paper is probably a reasonable compromise. (I use an expensive 100 gsm 'laid' paper for important correspondence and a 70 gsm bond for less important letters and invoices.)

In my opinion, the printing on a writer-photographer's headed paper should be very 'discreet'; I dislike paper which stridently proclaims that the originator is a writer or photographer or what-have-you.

My own note-paper has merely my name and address on it. Some of my friends also include, in small letters, something like, 'Member of Society of Authors', or 'Member — NUJ', or just 'Photographer' or 'Writer'. As long as this is unobtrusive it is acceptable — but in my view it is usually unnecessary; such 'qualifications' as I have can always, if necessary, be made apparent within the letter.

In the past, I have found it useful to have reply envelopes printed with my name and address. Every time I submit an article, I need (*see* Chapter 5) to enclose a stamped addressed envelope. So I had some printed. (I needed them anyway, for gathering responses to a questionnaire relating to a book I was writing.)

Another, possibly better idea (I am thinking about it for my next printing order), is to have printed sticky labels; these should though, in my view, be larger than the usual 'back of envelope stickers'. The ordinary, small labels are essential anyway — for photograph backs and for envelope sealing.

Invoices sometimes worry beginner writer-photographers. They need not. First, you shouldn't send one unless you know that the editor requires an invoice. (They will tell you, the first time you 'chase' an overly late payment.) Secondly, typed on your headed note-paper, it need say no more than something like:

00 March 19—

INVOICE

The Editor
Mudshire Life
23 High Street
Muddlecombe Mudds MM9 6XX

To:

Article 'TITLE' 1000 words, with 6 black and
white photographs, used in Mudshire Life in
[insert date of issue if known, otherwise leave
blank for editorial completion]   £. . . .
   [Leave the payment amount blank unless
you know — the editor will complete as
appropriate.]

TOTAL DUE   £. . . .

(Note: No VAT registration)

Keep a copy of your invoice — and make a point of
checking periodically for unpaid invoices. That's being
business-like.

7

INTO COLOUR

Throughout this book we have made the point that the 'ordinary' — and certainly the beginning — writer-photographer should take photographs exclusively in black and white. This is undoubtedly correct.

But the situation is changing: more colour is being used all the time. Indeed, there is already a good market for colour photographs — but it is not one for the beginner. As the writer-photographer gains in skill and confidence though, the colour photography market is worth contemplating.

Let us consider:

- the present, and growing, market for the type of colour picture that is appropriate for the 'ordinary' writer-photographer — and some idea of how well colour photography pays;
- the different equipment needed, and film(s) used, for colour photography;

- the difference in the pictorial approach needed for colour photography.

But first, another warning. Do not attempt to move into colour photography — for money – until you are a really good photographer. Stick to black and white — and 'happy snaps'. I do.

The colour market

First and foremost, the 'ordinary' writer-photographer should think about supplying colour pictures for magazine covers. Even if a magazine uses nearly all black and white pictures on its inside pages, most magazines use a colour picture on the cover. And the local county magazine is a good place to start. (So too might *The Lady* be.)

The county type of magazine — and this can perhaps be extended to include the 'beautiful countryside' type of magazine too – frequently uses an attractive scene on its cover. The scene is usually 'country', but picturesque townscapes too are often used.

There is a knack (at least one) to photographing cover pictures: the most suitable cover pictures are usually those that make specific provision for the magazine title. Often this need be no more than a blank sky. But a picture with an important part of its composition across its top third could be rejected on those grounds alone. *Look* at cover pictures used by a 'target' magazine; notice how space is left for the title. Go thou and do likewise.

Notice too how, particularly in magazine covers that use a person or a face as the subject, the person or face is usually to the right of the picture, looking left.

The same tendency applies to scenery pictures — but is less noticeable.

The logic behind this imbalance is that the magazine title often *tends to the left* — unless it stretches across the whole width. The title's *left-tendency* is related to the way magazines are displayed on the racks in shops; many shops overlap magazines on their right-hand side. A left-hand title will therefore remain well-displayed. The magazine contents too — for the same reasons — are often printed down the left side of the cover picture.

If the composition of your cover picture is vaguely to the right, 'looking left', it could have a better chance of selling. This is, of course, not a hard and fast rule — hence my calling it a *tendency*. But look for yourself at the more popular, best-selling, magazines. You will see that, in this respect, I'm right. Not with every magazine, but with many.

It would not be unreasonable to expect a fee of around £50 (for a single reproduction right, of course) for a colour picture used as a cover for one of the better-paying county magazines. The bigger national 'country' style magazines might pay two or three times as much as that for a cover picture — but their standards are very high. And the more miserly of the county magazines might offer as little as £10 for a colour cover. This should be rejected, except perhaps, while you are 'learning'.

The same magazines — county, 'country', and 'nostalgia' — also take a lot of colour pictures (usually for decorative, rather than illustrative, use) on internal pages. These will be not dissimilar to those on the cover — but obviously without the composition restraints imposed by the title, etc. For internal pictures in colour, there is much to be said for the foreground domination suggested for black and white pictures.

Payment rates for internal use of colour pictures are lower than for covers. A single reproduction right on an internal page will usually attract around £20.

There is not yet — at least, not for the 'ordinary' writer-photographer — much of a magazine market for many colour pictures other than land- and town-scapes. And that market is largely confined to the county/countryside/nostalgia magazines. But that is no bad, nor small, field in which to operate.

(There may be a further market for on spec travel pictures in colour, but this is a difficult market to break into. You might manage to sell the occasional colour travel picture directly to package holiday organisers, for their brochures. In this field though, it is probably best to offer your pictures through one of the picture agencies. There are several agencies specialising in travel brochure pictures — and a few do not require the minimum 100-picture submissions mentioned in the previous chapter. But they do take their 50 per cent commission.)

The overall market for colour pictures does though, now extend beyond just magazines. Colour pictures can also be sold to calendar publishers, to greetings card publishers and to picture postcard publishers. Look at calendars, greetings cards and picture postcard racks to see the types of picture that will sell. (Much like the county etc. magazines.)

As for a cover, a fee of around £50 would be reasonable for calendar or card use. You will sell calendar and/or postcard rights only — NOT magazine reproduction rights. This means that having sold a picture to the card/calendar market, you may still be able to sell single reproduction rights in the same picture, to the magazine market.

Colour equipment and film

For your black and white photography, we have recommended that you use a 35 mm camera — either a compact or a more sophisticated SLR. And it is possible to sell colour photographs taken with a 35 mm camera. But difficult.

The county/country/nostalgia market for colour pictures, and the card/calendar market even more so, requires the use of bigger film than 35 mm. Not many years ago, you would not have found it easy to sell cover pictures taken on anything other than a large-format (say 5″ × 4″) cut-film camera. Today though, 120-size roll-film is almost universally acceptable. And this usually means 2¼″ square (6 cm × 6 cm) pictures.

If therefore, you are thinking of getting into colour photography, it is just about essential that you invest in a 120-size roll-film camera. And 120-size cameras are expensive. So think hard before you get into the colour photography business.

The ideal cameras for 120-size colour photography are either the Swiss Hasselblad or the Japanese Bronica or Mamiya. All three cameras are single-lens reflex cameras. The Swiss camera — a genuine Rolls Royce among cameras — will set you back over £1000; the Japanese ones — well up in the Jaguar/Daimler bracket — about £600 or £700; in all cases the prices depend considerably on how the basic camera bodies are equipped. (The Hasselblad is exclusively a 2¼″ square camera; both the Japanese brands offer either a 2¼″ square camera or an equally acceptable — and more economical — 6 cm × 4.5 cm sized camera.)

If you are getting into this business, you should take careful advice: go to a *specialist* camera dealer. And try the equipment out very carefully before you buy.

A cheaper alternative is a twin-lens reflex. You can buy an excellent Mamiyaflex interchangeable-lens twin-lens reflex, fitted with a standard 80 mm lens-pair for well under £300. This basic camera would be perfectly adequate for the 'ordinary' writer-photographer intent on getting into serious colour photography. I recommend such a buy.

The principle of the twin-lens reflex is simple. It is much like two cameras, one on top of the other. The top lens views the picture, and transfers it, via a fixed mirror, to a ground-glass screen at which the photographer looks DOWN. The lower lens takes the photograph. The two lenses are linked together, on a common 'board' which is moved in and out to focus both lenses. The focussing is assessed by the photographer by the appearance of the picture on the ground-glass screen.

For top-quality colour photography a tripod is also a highly desirable investment. Cover pictures must always be pin-sharp; this usually means small apertures which, in turn, mean slow shutter speeds — hence a tripod. And because 120-size cameras seldom include the automatic exposure metering of their more sophisticated 35 mm cousins, you will also need an exposure meter.

We have already mentioned the need to use 120-size film for colour photography — at least for covers and cards/calendars. We have not yet mentioned the type of film.

Colour negative film, of the type used by the millions

of 'happy snappers', is not favoured by magazines and other markets. If you are to sell your colour pictures you must take colour *transparencies* (slides). In the 120-size, the most commonly available colour transparency film is Kodak Ektachrome. This has to be processed specially; there are many specialist colour processing services who will do this.

If you are taking 35 mm colour with the expectation or hope of selling your pictures, you should use 35 mm Kodachrome film. (Don't hold your breath though, it's a very difficult market. Stick to 'pretty' pictures on 120 film.) Other 35 mm films may be acceptable — but Kodachrome is more so, because it is the standard against which all other 35 mm colour transparency films are measured. Ideally, use Kodachrome 25 — but this is very slow; Kodachrome 64 is almost always acceptable. (The numbers reflect the film speed — in ISO/ASA.)

Having effectively dismissed colour negative film above as only fit for 'happy snaps', it does have one important market. There are many colour photography competitions; and these almost always ask for colour prints — ie from colour negative film. It therefore pays to be prepared to take pictures on 35 mm colour negative film for competitions. (Of course, to be truly prepared, entails a camera loaded at all times with colour negative film. This is a luxury few of us can afford. But I always have colour film in my camera bag.)

I generally use Truprint colour film. I am well content with their processing of my happy snaps — and the film and their processing will be perfectly adequate should I ever find a potential competition picture. And it's very good value for money.

Taking colour pictures

We have mentioned the importance and impact of strong, and often cross or back, lighting in black and white photography. The requirements of colour photography are rather different. The colour within the scene can itself often suffice to 'make' the picture.

For many colour photographs, simple, direct, 'non-constrasty', lighting may well be best. Deep shadows, so useful in black and white photography can sometimes, in colour pictures, take on an unexpected and unwanted hue.

In colour photography, the photographer should first consider the harmony and/or the contrast of the colours themselves. Think of a circle, with coloured segments. The colours follow those of the rainbow: red, orange, yellow, green, blue, violet — and back to red. Colours next to each other in that segmented circle will always harmonise well together; 'opposite' colours — ie, those separated by a couple of other segments will balance each other; colours separated by one or three segments may appear disharmonious.

Thus, a picture made up of orange and yellow tints will have a unified overall appearance; so too does a green and blue picture. If you set an orange subject against a plain blue background, the subject will stand out, but not appear too 'contrasty' — the colours tend to balance each other. Unadulterated red against a solid blue however will be a very strong contrast. But this may be what you want.

This concept of unifying, balancing or contrasting colours is all very well in theory. In practice, a scene will often contain a whole palette-full of contrasting colours. But an awareness of the effect of different colours may help you to avoid unintentional effects.

Certainly, if photographing a still life (an artefact perhaps) you can bear in mind the concept of the colour circle. Choose your background with care.

Misty, pastel-hued scenes may be highly evocative and harmoniously artistic. They are, however, less likely to sell for a magazine cover; nor indeed for an internal page. Most editors prefer the strength and impact of more positive colours.

For the county/country/nostalgia press generally, stick to good old sunlight. Emulate the photographer of the calendar on your office or kitchen wall. Go for strong, instantly appealing, images and avoid the 'artistic'. Except for your own pleasure.

Finally, do not expect to sell a lot of colour pictures. For some years yet, the mainstay of the 'ordinary' writer-photographer will almost certainly continue to be black and white pictures accompanying feature articles. But the occasional colour sale will pay for a lot of typing paper and rebounding stamped addressed envelopes. And a colour picture looks terrific in your scrapbook of published work.

INDEX

154